Z

B)

Buddha late
than never

26/3/15

Enjoy the read and your
Dharma practices.

Paul

Buddha late than never

Transforming Adversity (with Wisdom)

from Fear, Fantasy and Failure
to Freedom and Fulfilment

by
Paul Webb

Buddha Late than Never
Transforming Adversity (with Wisdom)
© Paul Webb, 2013
ISBN 978-0-9928283-0-1

Published by: Paul Webb Publications
website: www.buddhalatethannever.com
email: paul@buddhalatethannever.com

Testimonials

This book is just one great read from start to finish. Although it's Paul's autobiography, I actually felt that he was writing about my life too. It connected with me in a way that very few books have done in the past, and is refreshingly honest, courageous and uplifting. It confirmed to me that essentially our lives are defined by the quality of relationships that we have, and our first relationship has to be with ourselves. Get that right and everything else falls into place. Buy it, read it, and then read it again – you won't regret it.

Mike Shinton, Time to Grow
www.timetogrow.me

This book, and its content reflects the author well. BALLS OF STEEL. Thought provoking story that compels you to reflect on your own life and relationships in a way that resembles being hit in the face with a velvet boxing glove... A great read.

David Hyner Fpsa, Stretch Development Ltd
www.stretchdevelopment.com

Every so often you read a book that hits you immediately as sincere, genuine, riveting yet also informative. Paul's book does all these things in equal measure. Not only is it a fascinating read of someone's life, their trials and tribulations, it sets out to share Paul's learning from situations both good and not so good. I really believe everyone should read this book and help us all to recognise that sometimes we just have to talk about things and not hold back for fear – facing a fear sets you free.

Peter Roper Fpsa, Positive Ground Ltd
Best-selling Author, Award winning speaker and Past president of the Professional Speaking Association
www.positiveground.co.uk

Buddha Late Than Never is a beautiful book. For the most part it is beautiful in its' simplicity and ordinariness. It is a straight forward account of one man's journey through the joys and heartbreaks of life. Profound Buddhist wisdom applied to many of Paul's adventures adds depth and insight for those who know that we do not see the world as it is but rather we see the world as we are.

Miguel Dean, Youth Training and Development
Author of Stepping Stones in the Mist
www.migueldean.co.uk   www.steppingstonesinthemist.com

Acknowledgements

This book acknowledges the wisdom of many philosophers and spiritual teachers. In particular the teachings (Dharma) of Buddha Shakyamuni have been a great source of inspiration to me, both for this book and throughout the whole of my recent life.

Also, the power of meditation is fully appreciated. Without this my life would have been less enjoyable, there would have been more barriers to understanding wisdom and this book would not have been possible.

I would also like to thank the following people:

My mother, Lindsey Stone, Moss Westwood and Alyson Weickert for the proof-reading and critical comments.

Peter Roper, Mike Shinton, David Hyner and Miguel Dean for their reviews, testimonials, critical comments and advice.

Thanks also to the Fallen Angel bakery and coffee shop in Harborne, makers of the best "rocky road" in Birmingham. I spent many hours drinking coffee and eating there while writing this book.

Disclaimer

The stories, events and characters in this book are based on my life. Most of the names of people have been changed to respect their privacy. Where people have consented I have retained their real first names or commonly used nicknames.

I have tried not to hurt anyone or cause any offence. I have reported all events as fairly as I can and as I perceive them to have occurred. As is inevitable, the perceptions of others may differ.

I have also tried to avoid judging or criticising anyone. Similarly, I have tried to avoid saying anything of a hurtful or personal nature. In some instances, I have criticised actions people have taken, but not the individuals. Where my views and feelings are incorrect, in the context of (Buddha's) Wisdom, I have at some stage tried to provide balance by subsequently stating the "correct view".

The "correct view" is one that leads to a calm and peaceful mind for both myself and others. Similarly, it is without judgment or criticism.

Everything I have relayed occured up to the time of writing in the late summer of 2012 and by completion of the first draft that September.

I have done my utmost to do justice to the wisdom I have written about and in particular to the teachings of the Buddha. No doubt those who have studied deeper than I have would be able to improve the content. However, I hope this book adequately demonstrates that even with my current limited knowledge, I could have significantly improved my life and I have complete faith that I will do so in the future, providing I continue to study and practise Dharma.

My teacher, at the time of writing this book, a representative of the Buddhist tradition where I have done most of my Dharma study, has expressed a wish for it not to be mentioned in this book, in order to "keep its lineage pure". I have complied with this request.

To further respect its position I have, in the main, written about Buddhist teachings from memory, only referring to study material and Buddhist books to check factual accuracy. I hope this does not detract too much from accuracy or enjoyment. Other quotes have been gained from a variety of sources, many of which I have memorised during my own study.

Efforts have been made to fulfil requirements with regard to reproducing copyright material. The author will be glad to rectify any omissions at the earliest opportunity.

Contents

Introduction

1. Growing Up   17

2. My True Love – Happy Ever After?   47

3. Rock Bottom – the Only Way is Up!   89

4. The Light at the End of the Dark Tunnel   145

5. Life Begins at Forty   165

6. From Ambition to Purpose   187

7. The New Millennium and a New Direction   205

8. The Future – Going for Refuge   243

Epilogue   249

Lessons Learnt and Recommended Practices   253

Glossary   259

Dedication   261

About the Author   263

Introduction

It was 1979. These were negative and difficult times. The world was entering a very deep recession and there was great political instability.

The UK had just had the "winter of discontent", which saw it racked with industrial strikes, severe unemployment, high inflation and rising interest rates. Margaret Thatcher came to power in the month of May. The British economy was in sharp decline and soon there would also be confrontation with the trade unions. Whole communities were being decimated. It was all gloom.

The recession and energy crisis affected most of the world. The Shah of Iran was overthrown in a revolution, there was the environmental wake-up call of the Three Mile Island (the USA partial nuclear meltdown) scare and the USSR invaded Afghanistan. There was a significant threat to world peace and the atmosphere everywhere was one of intimidation, tension, concern and fear.

The mood of the times was reflected by two haunting pop hits from that year "I don't like Mondays" (The Boomtown Rats) and "Another brick in the wall" (Pink Floyd). They seemed to be songs about a state of mind that could justify mass murder and shootings as well as discontent in an education system and society, that could help cause such problems.

This negative atmosphere of these times and songs mirrored my own world and the turmoil in my mind. To borrow words from the first song the silicon chip inside my head was switched to overload. What reason did I need to die?

I was just turned twenty-five and had everything, or more correctly, should have had everything. I was embarking on a new stage in my life, to finish my accountancy qualifications and give myself a good career and lifestyle. The love of my life was beautiful, one of the best looking women I have ever known. She was a real Kim Basinger (the beautiful Hollywood actress and Bond girl) look-alike and incredibly she was as crazy about me as I was about her. I use the word "crazy" deliberately, for reasons that will be fully explained later in the book.

I was really blessed and had a great deal going for me. I wasn't exceptional at anything, but was lucky enough to be reasonable or good at most things. I came from a privileged background, had caring parents, went to a good school, had excellent health, got reasonable qualifications, was decent at racket sports and golf. I also had sufficient intelligence to enable me to go to university or pass professional exams.

Over the years, I had also attracted a reasonable interest from the ladies. Indeed most men would have been very pleased to have had such interest. But the jewel in the crown was Olivia, the beautiful, blonde love of my life. She was the most important single thing that had ever happened to me and I reasoned that no man could possibly ask for more.

Despite all I have just said, these were my darkest times. I was suffering badly. I was trying to start a new life at college, away from the family home, but was desperately lonely in my new surroundings and couldn't see a way out of my prison of pain. I had just had my first suicidal thought and was at my lowest point. I was also too young, naïve, inexperienced and lacking in confidence to know how to escape from my (self-imposed) hell-like dungeon.

What was the problem? Olivia and I were no longer going out with one another. We had split up in the summer of 1976. We had met again at a party a few months earlier, on the last day of 1978 and we were both hoping to be reunited. Unfortunately, neither of us actually knew if the other was still as keen on each other. Our feelings for one another were so strong that we feared rejection and hurt if our love was unrequited.

There should have been no problems. We were both crazy about one another. Maybe our feelings for one another were too great, in that they prevented us coping with the risk of loss and rejection. When we met at the party, a few moments of madness had led to a nightmare scenario. It seemed like everything that could go wrong did go wrong. Our debilitating fear had led to a self-fulfilling prophecy of hurt and rejection.

We didn't get to speak to one another or even to make eye contact. Olivia left the party very upset and was convinced I didn't care for her. Nothing could have been further from the truth. What happened next was a chain reaction of events that, to me, were of seismic proportions, and would lead to great suffering for both of us.

Nobody knew the truth except me and I had been so upset and hurt, that I just disappeared into my "cave" for safety. The more I got hurt, the deeper I would retreat into my cave and the less communicative I became. I can state accurately what my feelings and my perception of events were. However, I wouldn't be able to confirm Olivia's feelings or perception of events until our next meeting.

The above is what I believed at that time in my life. Olivia and I didn't communicate effectively, so at that point in time, I was just surmising that she wanted me, as badly as I wanted her. Unfortunately, the messages I picked up were mixed and were interpreted by a hurt and insecure mind. Consequently, it was my fear of further hurt and the uncertainty about her true wishes, which would be my main motivation and would prevent me from taking decisive, corrective action. It was fight or flight and I had incorrectly chosen the latter.

Negativity can spread very fast, like a raging fire in a forest, consuming one tree after another. So it was with this situation. The truth simply didn't matter. Knowing Olivia was upset and that she (mistakenly) thought I didn't care about her, one of my best friends had hit on her straight away. He had taken advantage of my predicament and her vulnerability. Many of my other friends and contacts had become hostile towards me or abandoned me.

That Olivia still had very strong feelings for me was evident from the extent of the upset. However, the subsequent actions taken could be interpreted as Olivia's love turning sour. My insecure and negative mind wondered if this was a perverted wish for revenge. I was simply so hurt that I took all the blows firmly on the chin. But this wasn't the time for me to act solely in a dignified manner. It was a time for me to overcome my pride and fear. I needed to communicate my true wishes and feelings.

It is when you are at rock bottom that you find out who your true friends are. I was at rock bottom and there weren't many true friends left. We had both been hurt so much that we needed positive friends to help bring us together again. Neither of us seemed willing to face the risk of more pain. Unfortunately, the necessary help we needed didn't materialise.

My own attempts at winning Olivia back were inept. We probably just needed to smile at each other and to meet up in private to discuss matters, out of the fish bowl of public scrutiny. However, I was simply paralysed by the possibility of any more pain.

It was clear that I couldn't continue living my life in this way. I wouldn't have been able to cope with any additional suffering. My loss had been enormous and I now devised a rudimentary plan to ensure I would never have to suffer like this again.

Over the years, I achieved the objectives of my plan. However, would I ever win Olivia back?

As my life evolved and developed, I found there were many philosophical questions to be answered. The questions I asked myself were:

Why did such a strong love lead to such great hurt?

Why would a close "friend", with so little to gain, jeopardise a friendship, cause so much distress to his friend and (seemingly) deliberately obstruct the relationship of two people who were deeply in love and wanted to be together so much?

Do (conventional) worldly pleasures e.g. drinking, partying, holidays, sex, money, careers, beautiful possessions etc. lead to happiness?

What are the true causes of happiness and suffering?

What is the role of the mind in finding happiness and resolving problems?

What conditions need to be in place, in order to find happiness?

How do we find inner peace? How are inner peace and happiness related?

How do we find contentment?

Can we rely on the mind? How do we control the mind? Do problems and the causes of fear exist outside the mind?

Is perception in the mind reality or illusion? What is reality?

What is the true meaning of life? What is our purpose?

Eventually, I found access to wisdom and the answers to all these questions. I hope you, the reader, will be able to apply this wisdom to your own life. Hopefully, this book will help readers find inner peace and true happiness.

I summarise the results I wish to achieve/assist from my writing with the well known prayer, which I have found in Buddhist and other texts (originating from the East), below:

May everyone be happy,

May everyone be free from misery,

May no-one ever be separated from their happiness,

May everyone have equanimity,

Free from hatred and attachment.

If just one person feels this book has helped them cope better with life, find some inner peace and happiness and/or given them access to wisdom, it will have been a success.

It may be late, as I am now in the autumn of my life, but may this book act as a "declaration of truth". May the power of truth act to heal and help all those in my life, both past and present.

1

Growing up

My childhood was only exceptional in that it was remarkably unexceptional. It was only after leaving school that my life became exciting and tragic, culminating in moderate conventional and material success, followed by a remarkable spiritual journey full of discovery.

I had what I now recognise as a privileged background. However, when you are young these privileges are not understood or appreciated, rather they are taken for granted.

My parents both did their very best for me and my two brothers, of that I have no doubt. I was the oldest, so I grew up very independent and headstrong. My mother had to cope with three boisterous (excuse the pun) boys, by the time she was thirty-one years old. Consequently, to some extent, I had to look after myself at an early age, when my brother Peter was born and even more so at the age of five when my brother John (aka Cab) arrived.

One of my earliest recollections was when, as a five year old, I was given a shopping bag, money and list of requirements and was asked to do the shopping. The shopkeeper gave me the food on the list, took the money, gave me the change and then asked me if my mother had "had the baby yet". I was simply confused. I didn't even know my mother was going to have another baby. To give a five year old such responsibility may seem odd these days. However, in 1959 it was probably not unusual.

I mention this story about doing the shopping, to help my heavily pregnant mother, purely to illustrate how my very independent personality would develop.

I was lucky to have two good parents. As was usual in the 1950s my mother raised the family and my father was the bread winner. I also got my values from my parents. I can remember when I was very young finding an old penny (when there were 240 to the pound) at a lido, on a hot summer day. I think I was about four years old and my father told me I needed to hand it in, because it wasn't mine.

I then witnessed a discussion between my parents. My mother clearly didn't think handing in one penny was necessary, but my father emphatically stated "he needs to learn...". My father was the winner of this discussion, so I went and tried to hand in the one penny at a kiosk where attendants were collecting money and probably selling goods and refreshments. When I tried to give the attendant the penny, with the explanation that I had found it and that it wasn't mine, I was a bit confused when he just shrugged his shoulders as if to say "so what". I then returned the penny to my father.

He was very independent, stubborn, determined and competitive, characteristics I would soon inherit. He was the only person on both sides of the family who didn't support the Baggies (West Bromwich Albion FC). He just had to be different and supported the deadly rivals Aston Villa. As we grew up he would take us to the Baggies one week and the Villa the next, but my brothers and I were always going to be Baggies fans. I always said that he took us to the Villa when we misbehaved and to the Baggies when we were good.

Although others didn't share my father's ideals, I still picked up his black and white views on what was right and wrong. My strong ideals of honesty and integrity are largely the result of his influence. Even to this day if I find myself making a statement, which may be of little consequence, but may not be totally right, I still often correct myself. I'm sure this is my parent ego state acting as my conscience.

Our first family home was a new development of houses in Quinton, Birmingham. Our cul-de-sac soon attracted a lot of newly married couples, who would all start families at the same time. Consequently, there were lots of children of a similar age in our road. There was a park and woodland area nearby. This was before the M5 was built, which sadly limited its use.

I used to refuse to talk to one neighbour Bev, a girl who was just one year younger than me, because "she was a girl". When Bev's mother took us to school I used to walk ten yards in front or behind her. Unfortunately, this behaviour rebounded on me.

By the time Bev was a teenager she was very good looking and all the local boys fancied her, but I hadn't got off to a good start and I don't think she ever forgot my childish rudeness. I never had a chance and Bev married a friend of mine.

My parents often comment that I was the one who gave them the most trouble. Interestingly, my paternal grandparents also said this about my father, who was one of four children. It was probably his influence that meant I would become very similar. I definitely became a "chip off the old block".

Socially I always found it easy to make close friends and apart from one notable exception, most of them have stayed with me throughout my life. At junior school there were my close neighbours Andy, Ant and Ian ("Inkie"). Andy would also go to the same grammar school and would remain a close friend for life.

I find I am drawn to eccentric characters and Andy is certainly one of those. At the time of writing, Andy is fifty-eight and lives with his eighty-nine year old mother. He works as a self employed transformer designer and his mother's house is a shrine to all the latest electronic gadgets he has collected over the decades. I'll devote a special section to Andy later.

At Grammar School there were Gaz and Ben (both nicknames). Growing up there was cousin Dave and my two younger brothers Pete and John ("Cab"). Additionally, in the sixth form there were Nick and John ("JB").

Nick and I spent a lot of time together from the age of eighteen to twenty-four. Nick was the youngest of four brothers, including his twin. He wasn't an identical twin and was very different in looks and personality to him. Nick and I spent a lot of time partying together, playing tennis and watching our beloved football team.

Nick was a bit of a Donny Osmond look-alike from the same era. He wasn't a high achiever like his brothers, but was pleasant and easy going. He got on with most people, but didn't really have a close circle of friends, so I introduced him to mine and he fitted in well.

JB was also a Baggies fan and like me was always keen to play football in any spare time. JB and I often came back from beer fuelled nights singing Baggies songs at the top of our voices. He was a great character and was the life and soul of most of our social events. He either invented or brought into common usage many of our catch phrases and sayings.

JB was a strong, tough-tackling footballer and we would often play together in the park and for league teams. He also played for the team I managed about ten years after we left school. JB was very distinctive looking and had very thick glasses, which I used to say were like the base of the pub ash trays of that era. He also had a good growth of whiskers and in the sixth form grew really thick Noddy Holder style sideburns, as was the fashion in the early 1970s.

Noddy Holder was the lead singer of the pop group Slade, who had a string of big hits in the seventies. These sideburns earned JB the nickname "Phones", on account of the fact that he looked like he had two telephones under his long hair, connecting both his ears with his mouth.

At school JB was quite bright and probably got similar qualifications to me. He had a great interest in history and like Inkie read a lot of books about war and specific battles. For some reason after school he lacked any great motivation to push himself in any conventional career. He tried banking and insurance but didn't seem to last long in any job. Before long he was working in a local store, where he was joined by Cab, who worked there one summer.

In the boy scouts there were Peter and Inkie (again). Inkie, also known as "Inkie Soldier" or "Inkie Helmet", was obsessed by the war and would usually be dressed in a German WWII trench coat and helmet. Recently, I have met up again with Inkie's childhood sweetheart Alyson, who married a Brazilian. She stayed with me for a while, when she returned to Britain following the death of her parents. We then went to a Buddhist festival together. It was interesting how our lives kept coming together.

Alyson recently reminded me that Inkie turned up for their first date dressed proudly in his wartime regalia, the matching German trench coat and helmet. As we grew up Inkie would organise all the local children into armies for mock battles. The gutters of our road were full of dried peas, as the craze at the time was to have "Sekeden" guns that shot them as alternatives to the pellets that the manufacturer sold.

At polytechnic there were Bill and Tony. Bill would also remain a close friend for life and would be the person who helped me most during difficult times.

Each of them would invariably include me in their social circle. Later in life there would be girlfriends and business networking contacts who also crossed the line and maintained close relationships. In addition there would be many transitory friends who would come into my life for short periods. There were many sources of such acquaintances from colleges, sports clubs, places of work, campaign groups, meditation groups etc.

Andy, Inkie and I were founder members of the Quinton Bachelors' club. Cab was later thrown out in disgrace, when he married, albeit to a Polish lady I introduced him to.

I was never lonely, but have become a social animal. Now I am self employed, I find I need to organise my social and work life so that I have plenty of social interaction.

Growing up, the major influences with hobbies, play and games, came from Andy and Inkie. Inkie would ensure there were lots of war games and playing with toy soldiers. After all, I was born just nine years after the end of World War II. However, Andy would ensure we were also influenced by science.

Andy was destined to become a physicist, scientist or electronics specialist. He would also influence our other hobbies, which were Superman comics, experimenting with our chemistry sets and trying to invent other electronic devices. I provided the balance with sport and football, but Andy and Inkie weren't really interested in football.

At the age of nine we saw the first ever episode of Doctor Who and I don't think Andy has missed an episode since. Like most of the children of our generation, we would watch Doctor Who from behind the sofas, terrified of the Daleks. It seems amazing now to think that those aliens with rubber plungers (due to the BBC's limited budget), on the front of their heads, could frighten anyone.

For my tenth birthday my parents took a few friends to see the War film Tobruk. Andy left the film well before the end and ran all the way home to see Doctor Who on the television. There were no videos or recording devices in the 1960s.

We had a "bring and buy" sale when we were in the final year of junior school and someone donated a transistor radio. The head mistress said to my mother "Andy will buy that" and he did. It provided him with hours of fun, taking it apart and putting it back together again.

At the age of ten Andy said he was going to use his chemistry set to invent a potion to give us superpowers, just like Superman. I believed him because, as far as I was concerned, Andy was already an accomplished inventor and scientist. I can remember how much I looked forward to flying and being invincible.

Andy had also been working on making his own robot. One day our teacher excitedly announced that Andy and his friend Norman had actually made a robot and asked them to bring it in. We were all aghast that Andy had achieved this. Then Norman walked in covered in cardboard boxes, connected by bits of string. I'm afraid it was all an elaborate hoax.

Andy is not in the least bit sporty. These days, he often comments that he is as fit now as when he was eighteen. He isn't boasting, he's merely commenting on how unfit he was as a teenager.

At school I once managed to dodge one of the inter house rugby matches and nominated Andy instead. I then went to watch him play and he only touched the ball once. Clearly, his strategy was to avoid the ball at all costs, but for once he was just in the wrong place. He caught the ball but quickly realised his mistake and looked terrified as half a dozen burley boys ran at him.

It was fight or flight. Andy just got rid of the ball as quickly as he possibly could, regardless of where it went. He was successful and survived. He was saved by the referee's whistle and a free kick was given against him for a forward pass. I don't think he was ever picked again.

Andy did go on to study for an electronics degree and is a very useful man to know. If anything requires electricity then he will be an expert on how it works. This includes mobile phones, televisions, recording devices, music centres and computers.

In the middle of Andy's mother's back garden is a ten metre aerial, a remnant from his days as a "radio ham". He is eccentric and very much a boffin. However, he is also a very social animal. He has a very easy going nature and is very kind hearted. As a networker, I now have a reputation as someone with a lot of friends and contacts. But I can't compete with Andy and I don't know anyone else who can.

I have been drawn to great characters throughout my life and people like Andy, Inkie, Gaz, JB and Bill certainly fit into that category. Many years later I would live with a lovely lady who would often remark that anyone who went to my school was "mad". I would say they were "eccentric" or "characters". However, I knew what she meant.

Nowadays my family often remark that I am "eccentric". However, I prefer to think of myself as "my own man". I have never been one to follow the crowd and have a highly evolved sense of independence. As I get older, I can see that I am becoming more and more like my father in looks and personality.

My father was quite an eccentric character and was very much his own man. Apparently, he was quite a handful for his parents. There are some great stories that clearly depict his personality and show some of the characteristics I would inherit.

When my father was young he was accepted to go to one of the better local schools. This was no mean feat for someone from such a poor working class background. However, much to his parents' dismay, my father refused to go to the better school. He had made his mind up that he was going to the local secondary school where his friends were going. No enticements or threats could make him change his mind.

Also, when he was young, my father had a bad accident, trapping one of his forefingers in a gate. The finger was a mess and was hanging off. His mother took him to hospital where he overheard a doctor saying it would be best to amputate the finger. My father then ran all the way home to avoid the operation and nothing could make him return. Throughout his life he would always have a badly disfigured finger.

Later in life, my father qualified as an accountant and successfully built a number of businesses. He was a very determined, competitive and motivated man. He also had a great sense of justice and fairness. This with the humility, from not forgetting his roots, helped provide him with excellent leadership skills.

When I was ten my father had a Rolls Royce, as a result of his business being very successful. He also had a business venture with the famous celebrity singer and comedian Max Bygraves. Quite a few of the local children were talking about the car and coming around for autographs when Max visited. However, the Rolls Royce didn't last long. To his credit my father, having come from humble roots just didn't feel comfortable with it. He even felt embarrassed going to the local fish and chip shop in it.

When I was eleven we moved to a lovely house and we converted the bowling green into a tennis court. The boys in the scouts nicknamed me "Mansion Man", but it wasn't that big. It backed onto some woods and the local golf course. Cousin Dave lived in a house at the other end of the course and we played golf most days in the summer holidays.

My father wasn't at all handy or sporty and we would often pull his leg about his few, rather pathetic attempts at DIY work. Unfortunately, being in the top class at grammar school, I did Latin instead of woodwork and metalwork. Consequently, I turned out to be just as poor at practical work.

One day my father borrowed a large lawnmower, the type that you could sit on and drive. We watched from my brothers' bedroom window as he cut the lawn. Then we noticed flames rising from the engine below the seat and the whole family could only laugh, as he realised what was happening and began to panic. Soon there were flames around his backside and he deliberately drove the machine into a pond.

I'm afraid the family just laughed uncontrollably at this spectacle and he returned indignantly with the comment "your mother would laugh at anything". Whenever my mother had a giggling fit at Dad's expense, he would make the same comment.

Although we were comfortably off, my father was quite shrewd at making sure his boys weren't spoilt, didn't think the world or anyone owed them a living and had a good work ethic. To illustrate this, as a teenager I was given one golf club for my birthday and one for Christmas, usually to the exclusion of other presents. Consequently, it took me over three years to acquire a half set of clubs. Similarly, to pay for the bicycle I wanted at the age of sixteen, I had to work for ten days at one of my father's shops.

My father taught me to value whatever I had. Conversely, many teenagers I knew were given sets of golf clubs as soon as they showed an interest in the game and their fad only lasted a few weeks or months before they demanded the next play thing. They were the ones who dropped out easily, weren't willing to work and didn't achieve any success. Ultimately, they were always disappointed with life and lacked contentment, always desiring what they didn't have.

Hopefully, this prior section will help you understand the greatest influences on my early life and personality.

My grandparents were down to earth Black Country, Midlands folk. The Black Country is an area to the north and west of Birmingham, which was at the heart of the industrial revolution. It is now quite a poor area and has been badly affected by recessions in recent history.

My father's parents ran a pub in Cradley Heath, famous for industries such as chain making. They brewed their own beer and sold "Webbs Ales".

My only recollection of my paternal grandfather was him climbing ladders to paint the outside of our family home. Unfortunately, he died when I was very young. Apparently, the doctors couldn't believe, for a sixty-four year old, how old his body seemed. This was the result of shrapnel from World War 1, working in a smoky environment and a tough life. His father had died, while he was still young. As the oldest of his siblings, I believe he had then needed to be the breadwinner in his family.

My paternal grandmother died when I was twelve. My recollections of her were watching wrestling and cowboy films on a black and white television and always giving me a chocolate bar whenever I visited. These visits enabled me to play with my cousin Dave. He was one year older than me and was like the big brother I never had. When I was eleven Dave taught me the facts of life, as well as any twelve year old can do.

My mother's parents were from Bearwood in the West Midlands and were also from a working class background. They lived to a good age. My grandmother died in 1984 at the age of eighty-nine and Grandad died in 1989 at the age of ninety-three. Grandmother would frequently look after us and have us sleep over. She was very kind and would do her best to spoil me, my brothers and my cousins Pauline and Geoff.

Grandad was such an important influence on my life that I will make several mentions of him throughout this book. He was an influence on my interests, such as my love of the Baggies, on my sense of humour and also with many philosophical quotes. He deserves these mentions of him.

Grandad was a great character. He was a moderate smoker, but kept himself physically fit and would have a daily walking routine right up to his death. All the local shopkeepers and neighbours knew Grandad and if they were interested in football then he would always stop to chat with them.

Probably Grandad's greatest influence on the family was to make sure all his grandchildren grew up as Baggies (WBA FC) fans. My club got the nickname the "Baggies" because they were the last team to play in the old baggie shorts.

We would listen avidly to stories about the Baggies and as I grew up I believed anyone supporting the other local professional teams was a bit odd. We simply couldn't have supported anyone else. There was one story about Sid Bowser, the Albion (Baggies) centre half, who Grandad said had turned up drunk for a Boxing Day match.

Grandad would talk about the great Baggies team of the fifties and their great half back line of Barlow, Kennedy and Dudley. Ray Barlow is generally regarded as one of the greatest Baggies players of all time and Grandad would continually complain that Billy Wright, from the local rivals Wolverhampton Wanderers, would deny him many England Caps.

Apart from Ray Barlow, Grandad's other favourite player was the flying Scottish winger Willie Johnston, who we bought from Glasgow Rangers. Grandad loved fast, tricky wingers who could dribble, get to the by-line and cross the ball. Willie could do that. Willie was also a great character and showman. He would frequently beat the full back for a second or third time before crossing the ball. I'm sure managers got irate but the Albion faithful loved him.

I can remember one home match against a great 1970's Liverpool side, when Willie was up against Phil Neale the England right back at the time. Willie ran him ragged and would keep going back to beat him time after time. On one occasion he went back to beat Neale a second or third time and using both hands pulled the top of his shirt out. Rather than concentrate on scoring or making a goal, he was just going back to call Neale a "t*t". The crowd loved it.

Willie was certainly Grandad's favourite player from the 1960s, '70s and '80s.

Between the ages of twelve and sixteen my best friends at grammar school were Gaz and Ben. We were in the top class together and always the three of us socialised together. More importantly, we were all Baggies fans. Ben's father would often drive us home from school and Gaz and I would often travel back from Ben's house together.

I first met Gaz in the dinner queue, when I was eleven. Gaz was with his mate Ada and we started chatting. I had a brace on my teeth and Gaz nicknamed me "Scaffolding". After that I'd often hear the shout, while waiting for dinner, "hey look Ada it's Scaffolding". Then in the second year we were streamed and Gaz and I were in the top class together and became inseparable.

"Scaffolding" was the first of many nicknames I'd earn over the next decade including "Spide", "Spider", "Webby", "Hype", "Pype", "Gary" and "Fleet". Later at Polytechnic Bill would call me "Neckbolt" or "Neck", presumably on account of how ugly he'd tell me I was. "Neck" then caught on with all his friends.

Gaz was always taller than me and had his growth spurt well before me, so we were a bit of a "little and large" act. Gaz was lanky, but decent looking and the music teacher nicknamed him "Handsome", which must have done his confidence some good.

Ben always had straight black hair, with a fringe covering his whole forehead in what I'd compare to a Beatles type mop. As a teenager, he was always painfully thin. He stayed like that until he was well into his twenties. Like me, he always wore a brace on his teeth, which did stick out a bit. Ben was for the most part a chirpy character and got on well with most of his peers.

I was always small and weedy and didn't start my growth spurt until I was nearly sixteen. In our early teens I think the three of us must have looked a bit like "Bash Street Kids" characters from the Beano comic.

Like me Ben could be opinionated and he was always frugal. When his father picked us up from school he would often play pranks on Gaz and me, locking the car doors when we tried to get in. Sometimes his dad would drive for a hundred yards or so, continuously stopping, while a smirking Ben would play his games tempting us to get in, before locking the doors yet again.

Ben was also a bit of a character, who lived off banana and/or jam sandwiches for lunch and chips from the local fish and chip shop most evenings when he got home from school. He was a real creature of habit.

Getting a lift to Ben's house already meant we would save some of the bus fare and we would often save more by walking much of the remainder of the journey together. It was a real treat for Gaz and I to share a Twix chocolate bar on the way home.

At a weekend I would sometimes socialise with the scouts. Otherwise, I'd often meet with Gaz. I have many memories of going with Gaz to the Baggies and Halesowen Town (known locally as the "Yeltz") matches. We also sometimes went to see Cradley Heath Speedway together, although Gaz was far keener than I was on speedway and this became his main sporting passion.

Often I went to Gaz's house to watch England play in the home international football matches. These were great times. We were twelve when England won the world cup in 1966 and I was thirteen when the Baggies won the FA cup in 1968 with Jeff "the King" Astle scoring the winning goal in extra time.

Jeff was a real hero at the Baggies, but was probably most famous for missing a sitter against Brazil in the 1970 world cup. My bedroom wallpaper was covered in blue and white stripes and pictures of the Baggies stars. I can even rattle off the entire 1969 team off the top of my head as I write now: Osborne, Fraser, Wilson, Brown, Talbot, Kaye, Rees, Collard, Astle, Hope and Clark.

My father gave me the same odds as the bookies that the Baggies would win the FA Cup in 1968. He said he wanted to teach me a lesson that gambling was a "mugs' game". We pulled his leg about this great "lesson". However, I never caught the gambling bug. The only other significant bet I can remember was winning promotion in 1975, when the legendary Johnny Giles was the manager. Maybe I should have bet more often.

We had our share of heroes. I think Astle scored thirty-five goals in one season in the top division, Bobby Hope was our midfield general (our Johny Giles equivalent) and Tony "Bomber" Brown became the all time record club goal scorer (from midfield). Bomber's goal scoring record for the Baggies was not dissimilar to that of the great Bobby Charlton's club record for Manchester United.

Gaz was actually named after the Halesowen Town hero at the time Garry Fleet. Gaz was also always playing practical jokes. I was sixteen when I went into hospital for a leg infection. I was still on crutches when I came out and went to watch the school sports day, only to find that Gaz had entered me for a number of the events.

Most break times Gaz, Ben and I would buy biscuits or crisps and eat them together. At one time, a few of the harder lads started regularly demanding we give them some "jammy dodgers", as "protection money". Gaz decided to take the law into his own hands and one break time took his biscuits into the toilet and peed on them. Gaz was very amused when the bullies complained the biscuits were soggy and they never bothered us again. Job done!

Gaz was quite good at long distance running and would probably expect to come in the top ten in the year (of ninety). I would probably expect to come between twentieth and thirtieth. However, the one year Gaz said to me "I'm not going to bother this year, do you fancy walking around the course with me?". I reluctantly agreed, but as we approached the school and finishing line, Gaz said "right Webb I'm not coming in last". I couldn't out sprint Gaz, so I came in last and got a telling off from the games teacher. Andy even took some photos of my rollicking.

Then there was Subbuteo, the table football game. This was the craze for all us teenage lads, where you flicked the players, who were mounted on round bases and tried to score in what looked like conventional goals. We collected different club and national teams in their traditional colours. We all had the Baggies and Brazil plus a few others.

Gaz and I organised our own Subbuteo championship. To us this was our world cup. My dad had the trophy made at work. I got to win and keep the very first one. In my world it seemed to be as important as Brazil keeping the Jules Rimet (first World Cup) trophy.

Our school had some great characters. "Diddy" once turned up at school with a home-made bomb. One section of the school was closed while the physics teacher tried to defuse it with police experts.

There were many stories about "Diddy" his brother and the girls they invited to their caravan, but no one believed them. Then one day "Diddy" asked Andy to develop some photos for him. Andy left them at home in his lounge to develop, unbeknown to him the stories were true and the photos were the evidence. No one knows if Andy's parents ever saw the incriminating "X" rated evidence or not.

Basically, we had a typical teenage up bringing for boys. We had football, games, excitement and pranks. We had everything except girls.

As a teenager, I went through all the usual teenage hang ups, it may even have been worse than usual because I went to an all boys' school. I went to a grammar school in Birmingham with an excellent reputation. My first year studying "A" levels was the first time the girls and boys combined classes, although that was just for the sixth formers.

Having gone to an all male school, I'm not a big fan of them. It left me very shy and feeling very awkward whenever I talked to girls. If I now talk to my old school friends they agree with my views about how artificial this is and the damage it does to confidence. Young boys may be prepared for the academic world, but not for the real world of human relationships. Put another way all the emphasis seemed to be on IQ and not EQ (improving emotional intelligence).

I was one of the youngest in the year and was a late developer. Consequently, I was also one of the smallest in the year. I was never going to be in the school rugby team. With boys, a lot of acceptance by your peers depends upon physical strength. Academically, I was in the top class, but was near the bottom of it. This added to my growing up lacking confidence.

Being small, I assumed I wouldn't be very attractive to the girls. Surely they would go for the big strong lads. One day, when I was about thirteen, Gaz, Ben, another lad and I chatted about whom amongst us the girls would like and why. When it came to me Gaz said "what do you think the girls will think of Webb?". This was a serious chat and I was very uneasy. I didn't want to hear bad news.

The other lads agreed that girls wouldn't like me because I "had freckles". This was devastating news and I believed it. It seemed that, I was surely destined to always struggle to find a girl. I was ugly as well as being small.

Then things slowly began to change for the better. I went to the local church youth club each Sunday night and although some of the girls made it clear they didn't like me, nevertheless I would get the feedback from friends that some girls did like me. Rejection and being disliked would always be difficult to take. However, I got my fair share of girls who were interested in me.

That year, when I was fourteen, I received two anonymous cards on Valentine's day. To this day, it remains a record. I still don't know who they were from. There were three possibilities.

I hoped one was from Helen, the best looking girl, who was always friendly towards me. However, the likelihood was they were from two other girls who friends had said fancied me.

This moderate success with the girls was more than I had hoped for. Then when I was sixteen I went with Gaz to my cousin Pauline's seventeenth birthday party. One of her friends was very interested in me. This was getting encouraging. Then I really had my growth spurt and caught all the other lads up. Now I was being transformed from the ugly duckling into something more presentable.

In 1971, when I was seventeen, I started going with Grandad to the Baggies matches and he went with his next door neighbour Doug. Doug would sometimes be accompanied by his daughter Sue. She was one year younger than me and we got on well. Unbeknown to me Sue was going back to her friends at Oldbury Grammar School and telling them how much she liked me. We were also becoming good friends.

Then at Christmas, Andy had a big party. Andy was a great socialiser and his parents' house was absolutely packed. Sue was there and she introduced me to all her friends for the first time. The prettiest girl at the party just happened to be Sue's best friend (at that time) Pam. Pam had long red hair, was very slim and looked great in her hot pants, which were now all the rage. I was smitten.

Pam and I started dating immediately and she was my first proper girlfriend. The girls from Pam's school were to become good friends too and I am still in touch with some today. One of Pam's close friends Alyson was going out with my friend Inkie, so there were plenty of connections. Pam's friends also went to lots of the discos Andy worked on. They also knew Andy's friend Tim, who was the DJ. I still go with Tim to the Baggies home matches.

Pam was sweet sixteen, but was more experienced with boys than I was with girls. She was very bright and went on to be the head girl at her grammar school. I was completely besotted and also got on well with her family. Her father was also a Baggies fan, so he immediately approved of me.

Pam said people often told her she looked like Lulu, the well known pop singer of that era. Her older brother, also a Baggies fan, had had some success writing and singing pop songs. His greatest success, as lead singer of the Flower Pot Men was "Let's go to San Francisco". He was also in the Ivy League, another well known local sixties band.

It turned out Pam went to junior school with Gaz. She said "I can remember him (Gaz), he tied my friend to the lamppost by her piggy tails". That was typical Gaz.

Pam was great and I had completely fallen for her, but it didn't last long. I went out with Pam for eight weeks, but then she decided she wanted to move on. I was very upset and went around in a daze for a while. I remember her sending me a very nice letter that said "don't worry, lots of my friends fancy you".

This first cut was a deep one. However, it wouldn't be the deepest. When you are seventeen, going out with someone for two months seems to be a long time, especially when it is your first girlfriend. However, I did get over it and there were always plenty of other girls and plenty of parties to supply them.

I have kept in touch with Pam and she recently sent me an email which said "do you remember when you were a teenager and all my friends fancied you because you looked like Bjorn Borg" (he is one year younger than me).

At school having male sixth formers attending classes in the girls' school for the first time caused quite a bit of excitement for the young girls. Quite a number of their wooden desks had "I love Paul Webb" scrawled on them. I was even questioned by my biology teacher as to whether I'd been doing this myself.

In our sixth form there were two very good looking girls. One of them, Ginny, was on the same field trip that I went on. On the Saturday night there was a disco. I preferred sport and played table tennis with a few of the lads. I also disliked dancing and had self limiting beliefs that I was a poor dancer and singer.

Ginny came out of the disco a couple of times to encourage me to join them. Later she came in again a bit annoyed to tell me to participate. I did soon afterwards and Ginny came straight over to ask me for a slow dance. After the disco was over I remember Ginny going back to the girls' dormitory looking back over the railings, with a big smile, and saying "good night Paul".

I thought Ginny was gorgeous and intended asking her out. I didn't and I can't remember why not. I was still very shy and feared rejection. I had a very good chance and didn't take it. Probably, it simply wasn't as easy as I needed it to be.

One of my friends married one of the girls from this year and she would sometimes say "you used to think you were too good for us". I'm not sure why she would say this, but I did wonder if it was because I hadn't asked Ginny out. I wanted to but fear stopped me. The reality was that I was simply still too shy and lacking in confidence. However, it never ceases to amaze me how people often assume they know what is in the mind of others.

All of these events and others were evidence that I wasn't the ugly duckling that I had assumed I would be. I was lucky. However, my lack of confidence would hold me back. In a few years it would result in significant self induced problems and needed to be rectified.

At school I had just crept into the top stream, but was always near the bottom. Ben was brighter than me and was always about half way, so making it to a good university would have been easy for him. Gaz was brighter than us both. He could pass all the exams without too much work and would always finish just inside the top third in our class, just behind those who were expected to go to Oxford or Cambridge.

Going to a top university wouldn't have been a problem for Gaz. On the other hand, I would have to work very hard to earn my place at a university or to pass professional exams. Like me Ben chose to go into accountancy, but gave up trying to qualify after failing his final exams once or twice. Ben never bothered to learn to drive and in nearly forty years has just worked for two accountancy firms. Maybe he just knows how to practise contentment.

Gaz chose not to go to university and instead joined a large supermarket's management trainee scheme. There he met his future wife Ann. Before long Gaz had moved into the export business and passed all the relevant professional exams first time. Gaz always said, he had never failed an exam, including approximately ten "O" levels, four "A" levels, various export papers and his driving test.

I clearly had a difficult task to compete with my peers and to achieve (conventional) success.

Freedom at Last

I had had a very good academic education at my grammar School, but it took me years to get over it. This statement is very flippant, for reasons that will become clear later in the book. Although, I went to good schools, I did the minimum amount of work necessary to pass the minimum number of examinations. I started to realise in my 20s that school didn't equip anyone with the skills necessary to cope with life, problems and the inevitable suffering we all endure at some stage in our lives.

Over three academic years I passed seven "O" levels and three "A" levels. My grades were mediocre, so I couldn't go to my first choice University. I could have gone to Cardiff University (I think it was my third choice) to study business. However, I chose to go and join a firm of accountants in Birmingham. It was easy in those days. I wrote to three firms and two of them offered me jobs. After discussing the options with my father, I elected to join a four partner firm.

My father had been quite astute, in guiding my career. He was quite a visionary businessman. Back in the early 1970s he advised me that computers would soon revolutionise business. However, he thought that there would always be a need for accountants and that accountancy would always provide a good income, career and lifestyle. He was right of course.

Before joining the chosen firm of accountants, I had to go to Birmingham Polytechnic to complete the Institute of Chartered Accountants (ICA) Foundation Course. This is when my life really began.

The ICA course was for just nine months, but it was a very eventful period in my life. The difference between Polytechnic and school was vast. We had total freedom about whether or not we attended classes and ultimately there were few people pushing me. Basically, I had been thrown into the deep end of life's swimming pool and it was up to me whether or not I sank or swam.

I had one friend Mark from school who was also on this course. Very quickly I had met the lads from the Polytechnic football team and I was playing for the second team in competitive matches. I didn't excel, but like everything else in life I had sufficient skill to be a moderate player and if I worked hard I was capable of keeping my place in the team.

Soon, I would make friends with another group of lads, also interested in football, socialising and chasing girls. Pete,

Paul B, Tony and Bill became good friends during this period. However, Bill would remain a friend for life, despite us going in different directions for long periods.

Bill was a chirpy, down to earth, Black Country lad with a very positive attitude and a great sense of humour. We soon became good friends. He supported the same football team as me and amazingly was due to join the same firm of accountants. We were just two of four, from about ninety on the course who would join this firm. What a great coincidence! However, is there any such thing as a coincidence or were we intended to meet and become lifelong friends to complete our destiny?

Soon Bill and I were inseparable. While at college, in all our spare time we would be playing cards and on the football machines (rods). During classes we would often spend our time picking football teams with a certain theme e.g. the best "Baggies" (West Bromwich Albion FC) team of all time, the best Midlands team of the last decade, the best team of players with surnames beginning with "W" etc. We also both played for the Polytechnic football team each Wednesday afternoon.

It was during Bill's debut for the Polytechnic second team that I scored two goals direct from corners. In my unremarkable football career, that stood out as one of the few highlights. Bill was a better player than me and soon progressed to play for the first team.

Bill reminds me a bit of the England player Paul Gascoigne. He played in the same position, had the same physique, didn't mind the physical side of the game, had good skills and could dribble and score a few goals. Bill was very much a man's man and liked a few pints of beer. He was also always wise-cracking and joking. As we became great friends we would rib each other mercilessly and still do so to this day, but it was always in good humour.

Bill taught me how to play three-card brag and I was a ready learner. We played with old cards and I soon learned how to recognise certain marks and creases to identify the other players' hands and how to count when certain valuable cards would be dealt to me. Soon I would earn as much from the cards as from my student grant. The only problem was my pockets were always laden with coins.

The last term at college was the summer of 1974. It was the World Cup and Bill and I had a great time. Looking back all I can remember is gambling at card games, watching and playing football and tennis, playing on the football machines (rods), drinking beer and eating cheese and onion cobs (crisp bread rolls).

Bill had a certain type of intelligence. He was street-wise rather than intellectual, but he also had good people skills. Bill at college did what he always did and scraped through all the exams narrowly. With his positive disposition, I joked that if he was thrown out of a twentieth floor window, he would still land on his feet. Bill was never going to go to Oxford or Cambridge. He was a down to earth Black Country lad, with reasonable intelligence, a will to succeed and was very much a people person.

Bill in accountancy was like a fish out of water and by the age of twenty-one he would change his career and join the police. He eventually become a CID Inspector. This was far better suited to Bill's personality and skills than accountancy, which he soon found very boring.

Unfortunately, my lack of effort at college work resulted in me failing the exams. I passed the majority of the exams comfortably. However, I failed one paper badly and needed to retake them all if I wished to progress as an accountant. At this stage, I didn't really know what I did want to do for my career and in honesty, I probably wasn't mature enough to put in the necessary hard work. Besides, I was enjoying my social life too much, so the career was very much "on hold".

After we finished at college we stayed in touch. Bill also introduced me to his circle of friends and I introduced him to mine. We were both now inseparable and had a great social life.

Bill with his wise-cracking, good football skills, bubbly personality and love for beer meant he was usually the centre of attention with his school mates who all played for the same football team. Bill's legendary stories of college and "my mate Paul", meant I was readily accepted by all his friends. They were good times with little responsibility, much socialising and great fun.

Like most lads of our age, Bill and I would spend a lot of our time chasing the girls. We had moderate success and we would be involved in each other's love lives, with serious relationships just around the corner. Late in 1974 Bill phoned me to say he had been to a party the night before and wanted me to join him on a date with two girls he had met there.

I remember joking that I knew what the sort of girls Bill chased were like and said I'd better give it a miss. Bill assured me that these two really were nice and I agreed to go with him. When I met Bill I was shocked. He was right. One of the girls was Farida ("Fred"), who he would later marry. Fred was very attractive. She was very slim and had long dark hair and a lovely smile. She was accompanied by her friend Viv.

Viv was also very good looking and had long blonde hair and a good figure. I had a handful of dates with her. There was certainly nothing wrong with her, indeed most men would have fancied her, but we just didn't hit it off. Maybe it was just down to chemistry.

Soon afterwards Viv started going out with her future husband John. I suspect she had an eye on John while we had those few dates. Indeed when we met up for a date she would give me a list of the local pubs we couldn't visit. I believe she and John are still happily married now.

Bill was smitten and he and Fred hit it off straight away. They were married in less than three years. It wouldn't be long before it was my turn and I would meet the love of my life, also through the connection with Bill. Every Tuesday Bill and I, with often as many as a dozen friends, would meet at my local pub the Royal Oak.

Our Tuesday nights at the Oak were very enjoyable. I used to pull the legs of Bill and his friends, by making fun of their Black Country accents and they gave as good as they got. One day the juke box played the song "when will I see you again" (Three Degrees). Bill, his friend Neil and a few others stood up and started singing a special Black Country version for me "When will I sid yo' agin". We had invented Karaoke and everyone had a great laugh. There were many other Black Country versions like "Yo ay sid nuffin yet" (Bachman Turner Overdrive) and "the fost tarm ever ah sid yo'er faerce" (Roberta Flack).

One day in late 1974 Neil turned up with a new girlfriend Olivia. I didn't know it then but Olivia would become the love of my life. My life was soon about to change significantly forever.

Olivia was very attractive. Any man would notice that. She was only sixteen, but she could easily pass for eighteen or nineteen. She was five feet seven inches tall, had blue eyes and blonde hair and had a classic hour glass (35-24-36) figure. Although, Olivia was great looking, I had no desire for her at this stage. She was simply Neil's new girlfriend and as such was "out of bounds". I simply didn't think of her as anything but a friend's girlfriend.

Neil went out with Olivia for about two months. I got on very well with them both and I think Olivia was fascinated to meet the man who was the legend and focus of all Bill's humorous stories of college and "me and my mate Paul".

I liked Neil. Like Bill he was also a typical Black Country lad. Neil was a big strong lad, down to earth, with a few rough edges, but he was a real gentle giant.

Then one Tuesday in late January 1975 Olivia turned up at the Oak on her own. I remember asking her where Neil was and she replied "me and the big white chief are no longer going out". Neil being the gentleman he was had picked Olivia up for a date, been told the relationship was over and had still taken her to the Oak. He then went off somewhere on his own, presumably hurt and upset.

Before long it became apparent that Olivia was interested in me, so I offered to give her a lift home. Now the dynamic had changed. Olivia was no longer going out with a friend, she seemed to be very friendly towards me and suddenly I was aware just how attractive and likable she was.

After dropping her off I asked her out and gave her a quick peck. We had a date arranged for that Thursday. However, I needed to handle things correctly with Neil and respect his sensitivities. He would probably be told I had given Olivia a lift back and would probably suspect I had asked her out. Regardless, of what he might suspect I needed to do the right thing.

I knew it was only right to speak to Neil in person, before my date with Olivia. The following day, I went to the pub where I knew Bill, Neil and the lads from their football team would be. I was probably more nervous than when I actually asked Olivia out, but I needn't have been so. Neil, much to his credit, was a real gentleman. He said he thought that I would go out with Olivia, shook my hand and wished me well.

We didn't see so much of Neil after that. I suspected that he simply found it difficult to see Olivia with me. As often happens, Neil went looking for another girlfriend to take his mind off Olivia. He asked me to join him for a few nights out at night clubs and I did. I think he thought it might improve his chances, but night clubs weren't my scene and I wasn't confident enough to excel in that environment. Besides, I had now met the love of my life and night clubs didn't excite me anymore.

Postscript

As I write in 2012, Bill has just read and reviewed this section about us. In typical fashion he smiled nostalgically throughout. He then added in his humorous way and with the expected boyish charm, "you've only forgotten one thing, you forgot to say I was exceptionally good looking".

Whenever I pull his leg now, Bill tells his second wife Tracey that I was always jealous that he had the "gift of the gab with the girls". I just agree that it was true, he certainly did have the chat, but then I add "but when the lights came on it was easy pickings". The Mickey-taking is still relentless and hasn't changed in nature, in nearly forty years.

2

My True Love
Happy ever After? (1975/76)

Now for my love affair with Olivia. We hit it off straight away and I also quickly had the approval of her parents, who appeared to be impressed with me as a potential long term partner. They thought I was the best and most appropriate boyfriend yet. I came from a relatively prosperous background and was clean cut and presentable. They also assumed I would become a qualified accountant and had good career prospects.

Once I started to go out with Olivia, I found her to be simply perfect. That's not to say we didn't have a few minor rows, but if they occurred they were minor and were soon forgotten. She was as keen on me as I was on her and I simply couldn't believe how lucky I was. I can actually remember thinking that I had my very own beautiful partner.

I thought I had my very own equivalent of a Hollywood actress. Now whenever I see a young Kim Basinger, (the beautiful Hollywood actress and Bond girl) in an old movie, I always think of Olivia. I really do think she was that beautiful.

When I say she was perfect, I do mean it, but I'm not just making a naïve statement. This is not simply a case of love being blind. She was beautiful and we had a lot in common e.g. similar values, intelligence, interests and liberal political views. She was very tolerant, loving and caring and didn't have any strong prejudices.

We soon developed a tremendous mutual respect and trusted one another completely. There was simply no cause to distrust one another. So a big part of being "perfect" simply means being suitable and appropriate for each other.

I am now a big believer that all people have a perfect nature, rather like the pure blue sky. However, just as the perfect blue sky can become covered by clouds of various types, so can a perfect and pure nature be obscured by negative states of mind, resulting in negative actions. In this respect our pure nature could be said to be like a nugget of gold, that is covered by dirt. However, the dirt can be removed from the nugget in the same way that mud can be separated from the pure water that it is mixed with.

Examples of such negative states of mind could be anger, hatred, resentment, greed, craving, jealousy, pride etc. However, just as the clouds come and go, so do the states of mind change.

This is part of the impermanence of all phenomena. Just as there is room in the sky for the occasional thunderstorm, so there is always room for a few negative states of mind in all people. Similarly, just as a thunderstorm can't destroy the sky, so a negative state of mind can't destroy the true, pure nature of anyone.

Any problems with Olivia and changing mood swings and/or negative states of mind, or resulting negative actions, were indeed minor and were quickly forgotten by me. She was as good as anyone can be, certainly in the context of what is appropriate and suitable for me. If she had an imperfection it was the Carlos Santana records she played, or at least that is what I pulled her leg about. Otherwise, I really can say, with all sincerity, she was perfect.

A few weeks after we started dating, Olivia had her picture printed in the local Black Country Bugle newspaper as the

"Bugle Beauty" of the month. I still have a copy of this black and white photo, it was professionally taken by the newspaper staff and she looked absolutely gorgeous. The message she wrote has faded over the decades, but she still looks great. I had that feeling that I was the luckiest man alive and I was the envy of a good many.

I knew I was falling head over heels in love and remember rationalising, whether or not to hold back and protect myself from the risk of future hurt. However, I took the view that holding back would just result in losing out, so I had to take the plunge and make sure this relationship would last.

In 1975 the band 10cc had a big hit with "I'm not in love". Olivia used to joke that the lyrics reminded her of me and my "ladish" ways. The relevant bit was, "I hang your picture on the wall, it hides a nasty stain that's lying there. I'm not in love...". But the truth was, I really was falling in love with her.

Olivia's mom would also look after me. Often when we came back to her house her mom would insist on making me smoked cheese cobs. Life couldn't have been any better.

It was about the time of Olivia's seventeenth birthday, after we had been going out for a few months and we had returned late from a date, that Olivia said "I think I'm falling in love with you". Although, it was out of keeping with my personality, I immediately replied "and me with you".

I was so lucky. What could go wrong?

In 1975 everything went well. Bill and I played for our accountancy firm's football team. We had a good team. Bill was one of the better players and I played more than half of the games. We had a good season, narrowly finishing second in the league and were runners up in the cup. Olivia came to watch me in the final and I came on as a second half substitute.

In May it was Olivia's seventeenth birthday and my employer sent me to work at a jeweller client. I bought Olivia a silver bracelet with the inscription "Love Paul" on the back. The following month in June it was my birthday and Olivia reciprocated by buying me a silver bracelet with the inscription "Love Olivia". Everything was going well and I still couldn't believe my luck.

My twenty first birthday was on a Friday night. Olivia and I went with a few of my friends and they had clubbed together to buy me a Dunlop Maxply tennis racket. This was the same racket that the world's best players like Bjorn Borg were using.

I got badly drunk on lager and lime and vodka and lime and probably other spirits my friends were pouring into my lager. To this day I can't drink lime with alcohol. I'm sure my body has recorded the danger. Friends would take me and Olivia back home separately. She was very concerned about me and I was very ill the next day. On the Saturday, I had just about recovered in time to have a meal with Olivia and her parents.

I can remember one friend, on the Friday, drinking too much and making a fool of himself by constantly telling Olivia how beautiful she was. He subsequently apologised to her. There would often be incidents when people, acquaintances and even friends would try it on with her. Similarly, other ladies would sometimes feel threatened and act jealously. However, I couldn't fault her and trusted her implicitly. I never had cause to doubt her in any way.

I really was the luckiest man in the world and we were starting to talk about staying together long term. Was this too good to be true?

In the summer, things also picked up for the other love (and attachment) of my life, my football team the Baggies (WBA FC). We had had four poor seasons in the (old) second division under Don Howe. Then the Leeds United legend Johnny Giles joined as player manager. We started the season badly and after about ten games we were in the bottom half of the league. Then

Giles waved his magic wand and we went on a great run. Soon we would have a promotion place in our sights.

In the summer Ben told me some of the lads from school were starting a second team for their football club and asked me if I'd like to play. I wasn't a regular fixture in the works team, so I agreed to join the Strollers second team in the September. Now I also had a regular place in a team with friends. Everything in my life was working out great. It seemed as though I had a Midas touch.

At Christmas I bought Olivia a ring and she gave me a framed copy of the "Bugle Beauty" picture with a hand written message. In January we celebrated our anniversary and soon afterwards Olivia shared some news. She had chosen not to go to university, so that we could stay together. I didn't put any pressure on her and we hadn't even discussed the matter. She took this unilateral decision for the two of us and I was delighted. It showed a great commitment and sacrifice on her part. I was truly very lucky.

I think it was January 1976 when Gaz got married to Ann and I was the best man. It was a cold Winter day and we had to brave the weather during the photo session. Olivia accompanied me and we had a good day. My mother gave me a "how to be the best man" book and things went reasonably well.

Gaz was quite a private person and I think the only friends he invited were Ben, myself and our girlfriends Olivia and Elaine. I was honoured to be invited, let alone to be best man.

My only problem at the wedding was my lack of confidence. I was extremely nervous about the best man's speech and made a couple of mistakes. They were probably magnified in my mind and I'm sure they weren't noticed too much by the other guests. The biggest mistake was mentioning that the next speech would be by the groom's father not the bride's father. I even looked at Gaz's dad, who promptly told me it was Ann's father not him.

No doubt I went bright red with embarrassment, as I often did. Looking back at myself as a twenty-one year old, I would have to say that my biggest weakness was probably my shyness and lack of confidence. This weakness would hamper me throughout my early adult life.

In the Easter of 1976 Olivia and I went down to Cornwall in my Triumph Herald car. My parents had rented a large apartment and we decided to go down a couple of days before them. Just before we got off the motorway at Taunton Olivia took over the driving. Unfortunately, she had some difficulty adjusting to the ordinary speeds when we exited from the motorway. She ran into the back of the car in front causing serious damage to my car which was no longer driveable.

We had to wait a few hours for a local garage to collect my car and for Olivia's parents to pick us up and take us back home. I couldn't get angry with her and she was upset enough as it was. I remember us holding hands all the way back home and the next day we set off again in mother's Allegro.

In May 1976 the Baggies were completing their football season. We just needed a win at Oldham in the final game to secure promotion to the top division. I travelled up to Oldham by coach with a big group of friends and we got the win. Tony "Bomber" Brown scored a late winner in a 0-1 away win. I had even put a rare bet on us winning promotion at the start of the season.

Olivia and I would often tell each other that we loved one another and talked about remaining together. I just took it for granted that this would occur.

I have only made a handful of bets in my life, but as I cashed in the winnings I thought I really did have the Midas touch. I had a beautiful partner, who was madly in love with me, my football team was successful, the social life was great, with lots of friends in various circles and I was enjoying playing football and tennis. It looked like I would be living happily ever after, just like in the fairy tales.

However, life simply doesn't work like that. The external world will never work fully in accordance with our desires and wishes. Problems will always crop up. Examples might be sickness, bereavement, redundancy, addiction, investments losing value, relationship problems etc. Indeed, I was about to come down to Earth with an almighty bump.

Also in May, we celebrated Olivia's eighteenth birthday together at our favourite restaurant. Soon she would be working hard for her "A" levels and I've no doubt this was a stressful time for her. However, she was bright and confident and I had no doubt that she would do well. Then when the exams were over we could start planning the rest of our lives, or so I thought.

We celebrated my twenty second birthday in the June and then, ironically, on the longest day (21st) I picked Olivia up for a date. It was to be my worst possible nightmare and it really would turn into the longest day. Olivia had clearly been considering our future together and then she dropped the nuclear bomb.

Olivia thought we should split up. It was just before we were due to go on holiday together to Cornwall. I really hadn't seen this coming and was very upset. I dropped her off at her parents. Although it was her decision, she was in tears as she left and we had even discussed how we would get back together again, if the will was there in the future. As she walked away from my car, she started weeping uncontrollably. It was a very strange split.

I was devastated. My heart was broken and I had many sleepless nights!

Ouch, Samsara Hurts!

This was samsara and the big bang all hitting me together. For all intents and purposes, samsara could be said to be the negative world of suffering that results from uncontrolled, impure and negative, life, mind and actions. Every cause of happiness in samsara is also a cause of suffering. For example, having a beautiful partner like Olivia will also result in its own problems. But I still had to learn these lessons.

I had a very deep love for Olivia, but this was mixed with very strong **attachment**. If only I had understood this back then, but I was young and very naive. Pure love can only bring happiness, joy and peace. However, **we mix love with attachment and it is this that causes the suffering**. I knew I was in for a very tough time and told myself it might take until the end of the year to get over it. Little did I know how long it would actually take.

I now believe we split for the reason most relationships finish, a **lack of contentment in the mind**. Contentment is being satisfied with our inner and outer conditions. It is too easy to break up and the grass always seems greener on the other side of the fence. Olivia was young, beautiful, intelligent, confident, good company and was about to embark on a career and possibly leave home and buy a car. All this must have seemed to be very attractive and exciting to her.

Many (female) friends said we would get back together again. I also believed and hoped this would occur. However, there was always the chance Olivia would meet someone else, someone who was exceptional and she was certainly in demand.

I wanted to stay in touch with Olivia. However, I was hurt very badly. I was completely besotted with her and had had my heart broken. For a few months, I made sure I stayed in touch and I regularly bumped into her. However, it was tough. Olivia had clearly made her mind up that she needed a break and I reasoned that someone so young, with so much going for her, needed to have her "fling". Hopefully, she would later return to me.

I had quite a dilemma. I wanted to stay in touch to make sure I would maximise the opportunities to go out with her again, if and when she changed her mind. However, each time I saw her I felt bad. In the end, for the sake of my sanity, I decided I would need to break free and do my own thing.

I heard that Olivia's parents were very disappointed that we had split up. Her mother was apparently against her going out with anyone else. However, Olivia was very wilful and this simply wouldn't happen. I knew she would be determined to enjoy life and have her fling. I also knew that, no matter how hard it would be, I had to let her get this "fling" out of her system. Otherwise, there would be future splits, which would be more than I could bear. Hopefully, after her "fling" she would discover that what we had was a bit special and return.

Shortly after the split, Nick agreed to go on the holiday to Newquay, Cornwall with me. We had a typical lads' week. I drank far too much beer. I was told that a quite attractive maid, on a working holiday, fancied me. However, my mind wasn't ready for anyone else, she simply wasn't Olivia. Also, too much beer simply made me look silly. I was drinking to forget Olivia and I can remember one night peeing in the wardrobe, instead of the toilet and another night waking up upside down, in the wrong end of the bed.

Bjorn Borg won Wimbledon and we had a really hot summer in 1976. This provided many memories. However, I also had too many nights out drinking with the lads and feeling bad the next morning. Drinking only provided a temporary reduction in suffering and the misery would always be worse the next morning, compounded by the inevitable hangover. My life was now fluctuating between excitement and despondency.

I needed to learn how to control my mind. **There are no problems outside of mind** and my mind was hurt and I didn't know the cure. Most of the pain we suffer from is the result of how the mind reacts to external events. In my naivety I reasoned that I may have lost my one chance for happiness. I had believed the fairy tale that Olivia and I would live happily ever after. In samsara this simply doesn't happen.

If happiness and suffering are states of mind, then their causes can only be found within the mind. It is said there are always two darts (of existence) with any problem. The first dart, which is painful, is the event itself, in this case the split with Olivia. However, the second dart is how the mind reacts and it is usually this that causes the most pain. If the mind reacts positively pain can be minimised. In this respect, it could be said that **pain is inevitable, but (the extent of) suffering is optional!** Unfortunately, in these times, I had no idea how to control my mind and so I really suffered badly.

Samsara is like living in a thorn bush naked. Whichever way you turn you will get scratched. It is also said to be like sitting on top of a pin. We keep trying to adjust things (e.g. our external world) to make ourselves comfortable. However, pain always occurs. The external world will never be exactly as we want it and so we need to **practise patient acceptance**. Patience is being able to endure any circumstances with a happy mind. I had many lessons to learn.

Nevertheless, it doesn't matter how good your external circumstances are, it is impossible to be happy unless you have inner peace.

At this time in my life, I certainly didn't have inner peace. Nor did I know how to make my mind peaceful. As we approached the end of the year I realised I was still in a bad way and was missing Olivia very much. The six months target I had set to get over things was not going to be achieved.

Pam returns

Then during the Christmas holidays of 1976 I had a very pleasant surprise, when I least expected it. My first girlfriend Pam returned from University. She had just split up with her boyfriend of the last three years and got in touch with Andy. Andy asked her who she would like to meet up with and she said Paul Webb. Andy drove her to my house and Pam and I started dating immediately.

I certainly hadn't got over Olivia. However, I now had something to take my mind off the loss of the love of my life. My friends were also pleased. Pam fitted in well with everyone in all my social circles and friends saw her as a potential long term replacement for Olivia.

Pam was still a good looking girl with her long red hair. She probably wouldn't have been able to fit into the same hot pants that she wore the first time I met her, but she still had a good figure. She was also intelligent and liked all my interests. She even came to watch me play football whenever she was back in Birmingham. I have a great deal of respect for Pam and am still in touch with her today. However, she wasn't Olivia.

It really was unfair for me to go out with any other girls. I simply compared them all with Olivia and they always fell short. When Smokey Robinson came out with the song "Being with you" I would always think of Olivia and the line about "comparing each girl with you" was so apt. Would I ever get over Olivia?

Pam had an English degree, but was completing a teacher qualification at a college in north London. We would meet up every other weekend and in the holidays. We'd take it in turns for Pam to return to the Midlands and stay at her father's house or for me to visit her accommodation in London. They were enjoyable times, although I still longed for Olivia.

In the summer of 1977 we had a camping holiday in Bournemouth. My Uncle Tom lived there with his family. They had a luxury bungalow with their own swimming pool. Pam gave me a few photos of myself, which I still have to this day, with me on the beach and next to the pool. I always told Pam that the pictures remind me of the love of my life, but only because I am usually wearing a Baggies' shirt.

In 1978 Pam's father died. It was a bit of a shock and I'd assumed he was quite fit. He was another Baggies fan and we always got on well together. He seemed young to die of a heart attack and understandably Pam was very upset. I think he was just in his early fifties. My own father also had his first heart attack at the age of just forty-seven and he had continual health problems from then onwards.

My father had been a heavy smoker all his adult life and admitted to frequently having seventy cigarettes a day. He also didn't exercise much and had always been in stressful jobs, building up various businesses and he thrived on the excitement and adrenalin. The heart attacks occurred regularly and Dad's health deteriorated over the years.

One of my earliest recollections as a child was of my father having many late night meetings at home with his business friends. The next morning I would hate the full ash trays and smell of stale tobacco that seemed to fill the house. Certainly many of the rooms would be affected. As a youngster I vowed never to smoke and still have never tried a cigarette.

I have early memories at school and in the scouts of other lads persuading me or goading me to try a fag. There were often comments like "come on Webb, prove you're a man", or "go on Webb you're a wimp/fart". However, I reasoned that I was the strong one, the one with will power, for not giving in to peer pressure. As an adult I would often find myself judging and criticising smokers as being weak-willed and for having no character.

I had always had a fierce independence, now I would also develop a great determination. I think this came from my father's competitive nature. I was also the oldest of the three brothers, which again added to my strong characteristic of independence. Later I was to learn that there is a high degree of correlation between independence and success. Certainly, these characteristics helped me through my most difficult times.

It was a difficult time for me, as I hadn't got over the split with Olivia. Also, I changed my job in 1978 and I was finally maturing and trying to retake my foundation accountancy exams. It was also a difficult period for Pam, with a considerable amount of change. She had left university and split up with her boyfriend of three years. She then moved to London for a nine months college course, leading to her full teaching qualification. She then moved back to the Midlands for her first teaching job.

On top of all that change Pam had to cope with the death of her father. Her mother had died during Pam's infancy and so the death of her father was additionally traumatic. I think we were good companions and hopefully we were a source of comfort to each other during difficult times.

Pam and I split up early in the summer of 1978, just before the World Cup started. Pam sent me a lovely poem, the gist of which said that we would always remain friends, no matter how much distance there would be between us, how many years we would go without seeing one another or what changes may occur in our lives. It was a good way to part and I will always have fond memories of her and our time together.

It wasn't really fair on Pam, for me to be going out with her at that time. I simply hadn't and wouldn't get over Olivia. Pam actually once said that she felt she couldn't compete with Olivia's looks and that I needed to get another girlfriend as attractive as Olivia. I tried not to mention it but the spectre of Olivia always loomed over us and would also do so with all subsequent girlfriends.

I was starting to drift apart from Nick at this stage. He had been going out with a girl called Ann for a few months, but said he fancied Pam's old school friend Ellie. Pam arranged for the two of them to go out and Ellie soon became quite keen. I think Nick was twenty-three at this time and Ann was his first or second girlfriend, as far as I can remember. Unfortunately, Nick continued to go out with Ann at the same time as Ellie and his sole motivation seemed to be to show off to other lads that he had two girlfriends on the go.

Each time Pam went out with Ellie she came back badly affected, because Ellie was upset and we (indirectly) were responsible for the situation. This didn't fit in with my black and white ideas of right and wrong. Ellie told Nick I wasn't happy with the situation and when he mentioned it to me, I told him, in no uncertain terms, to get the matter sorted and to choose one or the other.

There was a bit of a pattern emerging, when I first befriended Nick at the age of eighteen and introduced him to a different set of friends; he started fooling around with one of the lad's girlfriends in front of everyone. It was a girl who used to chase after me, but I felt very uneasy with the situation. After Nick had left, the other lad turned on me for inviting him. At school the next day I had told Nick exactly what I thought of chasing after other lads' girlfriends, but Nick seemed to be completely insensitive to the situation.

One evening Pam and I had gone out to a wine bar with Nick and Ellie. At one point, I turned around to speak to them, while Nick was joking about how much he fancied Olivia. It was apparent comments like this were common. There had been other incidents like this. They didn't help my broken heart.

I also remember once going around to Nick's family home, during the time I was going out with Olivia. His twin brother came out to speak to us and said how good looking he thought Olivia was. He then mischievously said something like "and Nick fancies her". There was clear embarrassment from Nick and he had obviously been making it clear he fancied my girlfriend.

I never would see Nick as a threat with Olivia. However, it was clear that as we were growing up our values were not the same. I just assumed we would simply grow apart and move on.

In 1978 Scotland qualified for the World Cup in Argentina and Ally MacLeod, the Scottish manager, was building Scotland up as the probable winner and the Baggies winger Willie Johnston, as a potential player of the tournament. Pride always comes before a fall and history will reveal that the Scottish 1978 World Cup campaign was a disaster.

Early one morning that June, Grandad knocked on our door nearly in tears. Willie had been sent home in disgrace, the victim of a failed drugs test. He had taken a banned stimulant, but claimed it was in a medication prescribed for hay fever. Whatever the intention was it didn't matter. The World Cup was over for Willie and soon after for Scotland as well.

Willie was a great hero and really entertained the Baggies fans, although he would also often get into trouble for his fiery temper. He missed many games through suspension and I remember vividly one long ban when the referee got in his way in the penalty box. The referee turned around and Willie took a kick at his backside. Typical Willie, he said the only thing he regretted was missing. But he was a fast and direct winger and was Grandad's contemporary favourite player.

In his later years, I used to take Grandad to all the Baggies home matches. He loved it and waited eagerly all week for the next match. Grandad was famous for waiting for the car to take him to the game from about 1pm on match day. He would be dressed in his overcoat and scarf, ready and waiting in his front window.

I told Grandad all the corny jokes I heard on the local radio stations and he loved them. There was one such joke about the man who stole a mile of elastic. He was put away for a long stretch. Grandad groaned and within hours he had told it to the whole family. This was a typical joke that Grandad would love and his favourite comedian was Tommy Cooper.

I was to get close to Grandad in his final years and especially after Nanny died. He would tell me stories of how tough it was in the days before trade unions and legislation protected workers' rights. He actually said that walking home from work along the canals he often thought of throwing himself in. It must have been tough in those days when if you were a minute late for work, you were locked out without pay.

Newquay (1978)

In the August of 1978 Ben, Bill, Nick and myself all went to Newquay for a week. Bill was now married to Fred and Ben had been with his girlfriend Elaine since school, so they enjoyed their temporary freedom. Nick and I were single at that time.

I remember enjoying the holiday, but don't have too many recollections. I remember there was lots of beer drinking, as was usual at that time. On the first day, after a few beers, I fell asleep in the hotel lounge. When I woke up a few hours later I realised Bill had covered me in dirty magazines to embarrass me. It was a typical "Gazza" type prank from Bill.

Most days we played tennis, before heading to the bars. Ben always chose to play with me at doubles. He was still playing with my old junior racquet and was the weakest player. However, we had a good record together and Ben would inform anyone who would listen of our exploits and how long he had been unbeaten.

At Newquay Ben and I performed badly and lost quite a few matches. I took the defeats badly and after a few days the others chose to stop playing, rather than risk my moods worsening. It seems odd now looking back that I could place so much importance on a game of tennis. I have always been very competitive and these traits have caused a lot of suffering, as well as helping me succeed.

Competitiveness is just another attachment. I had overstated the importance of winning and had incorrectly considered it to be a cause of happiness, wishing then to achieve the desired victories. Although my competitive nature and determination to succeed would cause me some problems, they would nevertheless come to my rescue during the most difficult period in my life, which was not too far in the future.

The four of us got on very well and we all had a good week in Newquay. I was the common link. Ben was one of my best friends from grammar school, Nick my closest friend in the sixth form and Bill was my good friend from Polytechnic. However, there wouldn't be many such opportunities in the future as the dynamics of our friendship would soon change dramatically, painfully and forever.

1978 Bad to Worse

In September 1978 I started playing football for a new team. I returned from Newquay and wasn't picked for the first Strollers game. I was then invited by Bill to join his "Stompers" team and I already knew quite a few of the lads who played. Many of them went to Olivia's grammar school.

I now had more links with Olivia. Within a few weeks I did get an indirect message, which may have come from her. I'm not sure if the message was second or third hand, but one day Bill said "I hear Olivia wants to go out with you again". On the one hand this was the news I wanted to hear. However, I was wary because I knew I couldn't take any more hurt.

The last I knew was that Olivia had a serious boyfriend and I can remember replying to Bill "I don't think she does". Bill just said "well, that's not what I hear". I didn't say any more, this sounded like great news but I didn't want to build my hopes up in case I got badly let down. In truth my lack of confidence probably wouldn't allow me to believe Olivia still wanted me. Why would this beautiful lady, who most men desired, still be hopelessly in love with me, as I was with her? In truth, I probably didn't think I was good enough.

The Stompers' left back Pip was married to one of Olivia's best friends. On New Year's Eve there was to be a party hosted by Pip and Trish. Then I got another message from Geoff, the host's brother that Olivia would be at the party and Pip didn't want any trouble. What did this mean? Had this come from Olivia? Did she want to avoid me and not be pestered by me? All along I received mixed messages and my insecure mind would always interpret them by assuming the worst case scenario and wishing to avoid further hurt beyond all else.

The big day of the party arrived. Olivia and I had hardly spoken for two years and I was really nervous. I already had a broken heart and I assumed Olivia would be at the party with her boyfriend. I knew it was going to be hard.

I had put Bill's comments out of my mind, so as not to build up my hopes. My plan was just to get through the evening, be polite and basically just survive, without giving any possible cause for bad feeling to arise.

To my surprise Olivia turned up later with a female friend and no boyfriend. She was at one end of the lounge and I was at the other end. I tried to make eye contact and smile at her, in the hope of breaking the ice. I didn't want any distractions and for once in my life, I certainly didn't want any other women chasing me.

Soon after Olivia had arrived I caught the eye of the host Trish. Trish smiled and just said go and talk to Olivia. I just smiled back. Did this mean Olivia still wanted me?

I then had a reaction which was to form a pattern. My initial and immediate reaction was one of fear (of rejection). Within a few seconds I wanted to ask Trish to take me across the room to talk to Olivia. But by the time I tried to speak to Trish she was engrossed in a conversation with another guest. This was the first of many lost opportunities.

The immediate response is always the emotional one. In my case fear was to constantly overrule the wish to express my true feelings and to open up and speak truth, especially to others. It was the first of many opportunities lost and I have subsequently repented at my leisure.

As the evening progressed a young lady, whose name I can't remember, did pursue me. On another occasion I might have been interested, but not on this night. I was trying to subtly catch Olivia's attention and this other lady must have thought I was eyeing her up. She approached me and we chatted for a while.

It was just the usual small talk, but then she asked me to dance. I said that if she didn't mind, it really wasn't a good time. I explained that a former girlfriend was there and said I didn't want anything to happen that could possibly cause any problems. She asked me to point Olivia out and I did.

I told this lady, who was becoming increasingly persistent, that I didn't want to dance with her, on at least three or four occasions. She then said "come on, no one would get upset at one dance". How wrong this would prove to be. I reluctantly said "ok, but just one". I then planned to make my apologies at the end of the dance and politely move on, back to trying to catch Olivia's attention.

I went to put the drinks down and turned around to find Olivia sitting in a chair just a few feet from this lady. Olivia had her back to me, so I couldn't make eye contact and smile at her. I walked slowly towards the other lady and reasoned that if Olivia was trying to make contact, she would say something. Everything then happened instinctively. A few seconds of madness, that of all the events in my life, would have by far the greatest impact.

I was between the "devil and the deep blue sea". It was a difficult scenario. If I danced with the other lady, I risked upsetting Olivia and if I spoke to Olivia, turning my back on the other lady, then I would be rude to the other lady and would probably upset her. I couldn't win and anyway I wasn't certain whether Olivia still had strong feelings for me or not.

As I walked past, Olivia said nothing, but I stumbled and found myself standing in front of the other lady. I assume Olivia must have stuck a foot out. Was this some sort of desperate lunge to attract my attention? I couldn't dance with the other lady, right in front of Olivia. It would have been like a "red rag to a bull", so I made my apologies and said I needed the toilet.

I had needed to make a split second decision and get out of this situation to recoup my thoughts and reckoned that if Olivia was trying to make contact then she would follow me, away from the intrusion of the other lady. Unfortunately, Olivia didn't know I'd been trying to rid myself of the other lady.

Olivia and I hadn't spoken a word to each other or even made eye contact. It then went from bad to worse. There must have been some sort of upset and/or scene. I don't know exactly what happened because I was in the toilet at the time. I just remember an irritated Bill coming up the stairs saying "come on we're going". I was either being whisked away or thrown out.

Those few seconds were the worst of my life and certainly had the most destructive impact. My intention had been pure, but it obviously looked bad and Olivia had jumped to the wrong conclusion. I had acted instinctively in two or three seconds of madness and had tried to extricate myself from the situation, so that I could talk to Olivia. Presumably she thought I was snubbing her and going off with another woman.

Things aren't always as they appear and they certainly weren't in this case. However, I had been inept in my (beer affected) handling of this situation. I certainly hadn't had too much to drink. However, I had had three or four pints and that may have affected my thinking and reactions. Nervousness, beer and fear hadn't helped.

There was no time to speak to the hosts or anything. As we left the party, our group were already prepared for the getaway and were waiting in the car. It had all happened very quickly and decisively. The incident must have been significant and I'm sure everyone thought I'd done something despicable. A female friend said "well you got another lady and Olivia didn't get another man". I wanted to put the matter straight, but in a state of shock just muttered something vague like "it's not what I wanted".

❧

Reconciliation?

After the party, I was upset myself but assumed that when everything had died down that Olivia would send me some sort of message. Hopefully, it would be something positive like "she's still very fond of you" or "she wants to talk with you". Unfortunately, there was no message!

The next day I saw Nick. Apparently, he had bumped into Olivia in a wine bar before the party. Was this a coincidence? Is there such a thing as a coincidence or was I about to have the biggest and most difficult lesson of my life?

Nick said with a smile, "so you saw Olivia last night, didn't you?". I assumed, from his manner, that he expected us to be together again, but I don't know what Olivia had said to him. I just shook my head and looked up to the ceiling indicating that things hadn't gone well, that I had a problem to resolve and also indicating my annoyance at effectively being thrown out of the party.

Nick's response was astonishing. I expected him to look surprised and to ask me what had happened. However, he said nothing. He just looked away with a smile on his face. He was unconcerned with our problem or with helping us. I knew then that I couldn't trust him.

Regardless of what Nick was planning, I didn't think it mattered. I knew the depth of Olivia's feelings for me while we were going out and that she only thought of Nick as a likeable friend. In sporting terms Olivia was "mine to lose". In some ways, if Nick did fancy his chances with Olivia, it would be good for him to make his move and to be told by Olivia that she was only interested in him as a friend.

After this Nick's behaviour became increasingly strange and he would soon be avoiding any contact with me completely. A few days after the party we had a football team disco that I had organised. I phoned Nick, but he was trying to wriggle out of going. As he couldn't come up with a good excuse he did attend.

I was hoping that Pip and Trish had sold a ticket to Olivia and that she would be there. There had been a bad atmosphere after the party, so I felt I couldn't ask the question. I hoped I would be able to explain things to Olivia and resolve the issues. Unfortunately, Olivia wasn't there. Pip returned two tickets that were unused but paid for. I assumed that these had belonged to Olivia and her (former?) boyfriend.

Shortly after the disco I went to a packed wine bar in Birmingham with a female companion. We saw Nick going to the toilet, but again he acted very strangely and was evasive. He said he was leaving but wouldn't say who he was with or where he was going. That would be the last time I saw Nick for quite a few years.

By now my friends were deserting me, there was no message from Olivia and I was in a bad way.

Unfortunately, I was being deafened by silence!

The only thing that was going well at that time was the Baggies (WBA FC). We had just beaten both Arsenal (2-1) and Manchester United (5-3) in consecutive away matches, in absolutely brilliant fashion. We were in excellent form.

The Baggies had a great team at that time and were second in the top division, behind Liverpool. These were the days of Bryan Robson, Tony Brown, Willie Johnston and the "Three Degrees" Brendon Batson, Cyrille Regis and the late Laurie Cunningham. The Baggies manager Ron Atkinson affectionately called Batson, Regis and Cunningham the "Three Degrees", because we were the first top flight club to have three black players in the team.

Shortly after the fateful party, in January 1979, the Baggies were due to play at Anfield, home of the legendary Liverpool team. This was one of the biggest matches in their history. We were playing superbly and a win would give us a good chance of winning the league. I phoned Nick on the day of the match. He wasn't there but I spoke to his mother.

What Nick's mother said shocked me. He had gone to Liverpool to see the match. This was a major shock in itself and

I'm sure he had never gone to an away match before without inviting me. But then she said something even more shocking. She said he would be getting back quickly because he had a very important date. Nick hadn't had many girlfriends and I'm sure he would never before have been so proud of one that he would have told his mother immediately.

This really pointed to the fact that he was seeing Olivia. It explained his evasiveness, odd behaviour and the silence I was surrounded by. To this day, I remain appalled that the moment he heard that I had got a problem with Olivia, he was hitting on her, regardless of the hurt it would cause and the problems he would help create.

This was a case of two former partners who still had deep feelings for one another and probably wanted each other badly. However, I had a problem to resolve in that Olivia probably and mistakenly believed I didn't care for her any more. Nothing could have been further from the truth.

However, Nick had just seen my problem as a "green light" to try his luck with Olivia. He then avoided me, putting a seven year friendship to one side, and hit on her. He seemed to have no regard whatsoever to the devastation his actions would cause or compound to the lives of Olivia and myself.

In many ways this was Nick's best and only opportunity with Olivia. She was clearly hurt and upset and probably needed company. Like me, she may well also have been at the lowest point in her life. It was also probable or possible that she was very annoyed with me, so her loyalty to me would be reduced. The worst case scenario was that Olivia was so upset with me that she was trying to hurt me, as some sort of perverted wish for revenge.

I didn't know what exactly was going on or what was in Olivia's mind. However, things were clearly going from bad to worse and I was constantly having one layer of hurt heaped on top of another.

Regardless of the morals and ethics, I still can't believe why Nick acted the way he did. At best the benefits for him would be minimal. He would probably be politely turned down by Olivia and at best he would receive a few scraps in the form of a few dates, due to the circumstances. These benefits, if any, would be far outweighed by the various risks and harm caused to others.

Firstly there was the risk I would be hurt significantly. Then there was the probability that Olivia and I would find it more difficult to be reconciled and would both suffer as a result. Our lives would probably be significantly changed. Great hurt and significant difficulties would be virtually inevitable for both of us.

The risks to Nick himself were also great. Firstly, he would probably soon be "dumped" and hurt. He would also, almost certainly, lose me as a friend. Similarly, if I chose to speak badly of him, which I never did, then his reputation would be badly damaged. Finally, by badly hurting me, he was likely to lose access to many of his social circles.

There would be no winners, considerable unnecessary hurt would be suffered and lives would be changed forever.

How could this scenario have been better with everyone being a winner? It's quite simple, Nick just needed to be open, honest and truthful. All Nick needed to do was ask me whether or not I was still interested in Olivia. If I had said yes and the truth had come out then Olivia and I would have been winners and Nick would have retained his friends. If I was not interested in Olivia then Nick would have been able to ask her out with my blessing and all friendships would have been intact.

However, I don't think Nick was ever concerned about my feelings or the long term future of myself and Olivia. Indeed his actions were those of pure deceit, suggesting that he was only interested in himself, regardless of how much hurt he would cause and how little benefit he would gain.

1979 and the Assassination

I didn't receive any messages from Olivia either directly or through mutual friends and contacts. Some people did start becoming hostile and aggressive towards me and other friends became very elusive, at the time I needed them most. Ironically, they could all have helped Olivia and I be reunited.

Unfortunately, I had been deafened by silence, but this was about to end, in the most hurtful of circumstances.

The message when it came was a dagger through the heart, delivered by two of the lads from the football team, who were obviously trying to maximise the hurt. After a match, they sat down at the same table I was sitting at, with others around, and one said to the other "right, tell me all about Olivia and that chap Nick". I just got up and went to the toilet. I simply didn't want to hear any more hurtful details.

Bill followed me in to the toilet, like the loyal friend he was and asked if I was ok. I instinctively nodded that I was. However, I wasn't. This was the most difficult time in my life. The hurt was great. It would take me years to get over it and talk about these events.

My instinctive responses to pretend I was ok were merely compounding the problem by sending out false messages to the world. I tried to act with dignity at all times, took all the blows firmly on the chin and didn't criticise anyone. However, what was actually required was a "**declaration of truth**". I merely needed to tell the world what had really happened at the party and express my true feelings about Olivia.

Why do men pretend they are ok when they aren't? Why can't they express their feelings and emotions when they are hurt? The more I was hurt the more I retreated into my cave, trying to think of a solution that wouldn't come, unless I opened up to Olivia or others. But this didn't happen; I simply feared further pain too much.

The main cause of all our problems is a mind that cherishes oneself, is overly concerned with "my" own happiness, freedom and suffering and puts "my" needs and wishes above those of others. Basically, we **take ourselves too seriously** and exaggerate our importance and problems.

Taking myself too seriously had led to minds of pride, in not wanting anyone to see how hurt I was and fear of more hurt. These negative minds of **pride and fear** had directly prevented me from speaking the truth and expressing my true feelings. It was the inner enemy, of my negative mind, that was directly responsible for preventing me resolve the issues with Olivia and obtain a reconciliation.

Buddhists believe it is the wish to be happy that causes us to be unhappy and to suffer. Similarly, **self cherishing is the cause of all suffering**. However, I had all these lessons to learn and at this time my mind was uncontrolled, causing me the most pain I had ever suffered. My "self cherishing" mind had created a prison of misery in my mind.

The message that Olivia was fooling around with Nick, someone who was for seven years regarded as a very close friend, was painful. This was the confirmation of what I had suspected, but wouldn't previously have ever believed was a remote possibility.

This incident was just more hurt. However, I can recollect the overwhelming sense of loss. I now instinctively had the realisation, beyond all doubt, that Olivia definitely still had very deep feelings for me. However, I had made a mess of things and winning her back would now be far more difficult, mainly because her upset may have turned into negative feelings towards me and/or a wish to hurt me. Had I now lost all chances of reconciliation with Olivia?

Not only had I got the problem of Nick and Olivia to resolve, but negativity was spreading rapidly and many people were being unpleasant or hostile towards me. Apart from the people from the party, word was spreading quickly of an incorrect version of events.

People, people everywhere, but not a friend in sight, or at least, that's how it felt to a very hurt person. I was at my lowest point and couldn't buy a friend. In some circles, people who I had been in regular touch with for years were simply evaporating and not returning calls.

Soon after hearing this news, I remember meeting a female friend who didn't know Olivia or anyone at the party. I needed to open up to a friend and I thought she would provide a safe haven for companionship. I was amazed when before I had said much, she just said "well you obviously didn't want to go out with her (Olivia), did you?".

If that message had come via Nick, wasn't he just justifying his actions in his own mind? Isn't it like saying "it's ok to steal my friend's money because I don't think he wants it"? Isn't it right to find out what your friend is thinking before trying to take his money, possessions or partner?

Word was clearly spreading fast and the rumours were incorrect. However, the damage was done and I couldn't change the past.

It felt like I'd been beaten up by friends and hung without a trial. Not only did I have to cope with losing Olivia, but it now appeared like she was mad with me and might be exacting revenge. I felt really betrayed by the former friend and those who had disappeared.

"Et tu Brute"! Caesar had been stabbed by his friend Brutus, as I had been stabbed in the heart by a friend. However, Brutus was an "honourable" man and didn't perform his act for any personal gain.

As soon as I had received confirmation I said to myself "right, that's me and Nick finished forever". This is not the "correct view", nor is it the most beneficial view. However, it is how I felt. Anyone who knows me will know that if I make my mind up about something then I will stick to it. As far as I was concerned, this was an act of treachery and betrayal. The genie was out of the bottle and there was no going back.

This dagger through the heart had been delivered by a former friend, who I felt owed me a lot. All the friends who disappeared during these difficult times were like the conspirators, who knew of the plot to murder Caesar and were complicit by remaining quiet, or actively giving encouragement. "It only takes a few good men to do nothing, for evil to flourish".

What was he going to gain? I couldn't believe his behaviour. I reasoned he was acting like an opportunist looter in the aftermath of a riot, taking from and heaping more misery on his own community. His friends, who were suffering after the fallout from the party and were in need of help, would suffer greatly. I had no insurance to help me recover, other than my determination.

Nick seemed to consider Olivia's strong feelings for me as irrelevant. However, these actions would merely make what seemed like a big problem become a nearly insurmountable one. It was to prove to be a very divisive action with no winners.

Olivia and I had frequently said that we loved one another and intended being together "forever". Nick's actions were meddling in two people's lives and were seriously jeopardising their probable wishes to be together long term.

If the problem I had with Olivia was a painful wound, then the problem could have been resolved easily with no lasting unresolved issues. The wound would have healed easily had I been able to talk to Olivia and explain how I felt about her and what had actually happened at the party. However, Nick's actions had opened up and enlarged the wound, to the point where it now might not be healed. His actions had been as though he was rubbing salt into this now gaping wound, creating much more suffering.

I don't know whether Nick was deliberately trying to make the "wound" bigger or to deliberately cause much hurt, but that was certainly the effect. I definitely suffered a great deal from these actions. I believe Olivia also had to endure a great deal of unnecessary hurt, if only for the fact that she had now lost the love of her life, which was me.

"Uneasy lies the head that wears the crown". I have found throughout my life that those with power, good positions, beautiful partners and wealth will be popular only in so far as they are in a strong position. Others will covet what they have got and will strike as soon as their position weakens. Examples of this are Tony Blaire, Margaret Thatcher, Ted Heath and numerous rulers and dictators around the world.

I knew Nick wasn't important to Olivia, but in many ways that just made matters worse. It meant either she wanted to really hurt me, or that she was in a bad way herself, or a combination of the two things. Their relationship didn't last long, maybe about three or four weeks. However, the damage was done. The stakes had been raised and my fear of rejection was increasing in proportion to the hurt and suffering.

"They shoot horses don't they"!

I reasoned that this could be a case of hell hath no fury like a woman (who believes she has been) scorned! Any hopes of reconciliation would always now be more difficult.

I took the moral high ground, comparing Nick's actions to saying "I'll help you hurt Paul and take revenge, just give me

50p". I also reasoned that, if my front door burnt down, would he be straight in my house looking to take my wallet? Was there any difference? Such friendships would never be the same again. The foundations for strong relationships, like loyalty, honesty, respect and trust, had now been destroyed.

However, there are seven billion people on the planet. What right do I have to assume my values and opinions are superior? Judging and criticising others did not and does not help. The most beneficial mind, for myself and others, is the one that forgives and doesn't hold on to resentment. As Shakespeare says, mercy blesses twice, it blesses both the giver and receiver. It is the same with forgiveness and not being judgmental or critical.

I didn't help myself by doing the man thing and I simply retreated further into my cave the more I got hurt. I didn't tell anyone what had actually happened, or what my feelings were and I was the only one who knew. My only strategy was to act as though I wasn't hurt. I was trying to kid myself as much as anything. In acting in this way I was simply alienating myself more from other people. I appeared to be uncaring and people probably just assumed I had deliberately hurt Olivia.

I thought I was acting in a dignified way. I never criticised Nick or Olivia. I just took all the blows firmly on my jaw without complaint. However, dignity didn't help. I actually needed to speak the truth and tell everyone what had actually happened and how I felt about Olivia.

Why is it that when you are at rock bottom friends seem to desert you like the guests on the Titanic deserted the sinking ship? It felt as though I had leprosy. Also, I wasn't in a fit state to make new friends. I simply wasn't in a positive state.

The situation reminded me of the murder of Cinna the Poet in Shakespeare's "Julius Caesar". Mark Antony, with his brilliant speech, after Caesar's death, had whipped up the crowd into a frenzy. The mob then killed Cinna, even though they knew he wasn't Cinna the conspirator. Whatever Cinna said they turned against him, on spurious grounds. The truth simply didn't matter and negativity spread and grew like a raging fire.

The justification for murdering Cinna was "tear him for his bad verses" and "it is no matter, his name's Cinna! Pluck but his name out of his heart".

In my case I was the only one who knew the truth, that I was still besotted with Olivia and that I had merely been telling another lady that I didn't want to dance with her. However, the truth didn't matter and people were simply taking it for granted that I must have done something despicable.

From that moment, I'd often overhear bitchy comments about myself like "he really fancies himself" and "he has a different woman each time you see him". Yes, there were quite a few girlfriends but only because I needed company and friendship (probably like Olivia, who I don't judge at all). The reality was I simply wished each girlfriend was Olivia. Just because you drive a Ford Escort, doesn't mean you wouldn't rather be driving a better car and Olivia was my Rolls Royce.

Not being able to open up and speak the truth was a curse! My problems with Olivia were merely the result of poor communication. It's so simple now. These days my rule is to **always speak truth** and to be totally open, but to do it **with compassion** (so as not to hurt anyone) and to not look for a result for myself (it's the ego that causes problems and division). Life is so easy now, but back then it was so tough.

Another excellent method for dealing with problems is a three-pronged approach, similar to the above concept of speaking truth. The first response is to speak openly about the actual issue, then to say how you feel and then to say what you really want going forward. This is rarely done in relationships and is the cause of many problems.

An example might be the lady snapping on a Saturday afternoon, "There you go again off to the football enjoying yourself". The man just scratches his head thinking "What is she going on about; I always go to the football on a Saturday". So there is friction, but the actual problem might be that the man has forgotten the lady's birthday and she feels unloved. This needs to be said openly, with a desired outcome achieved for both parties.

I think it was Martin Luther King who said "the truth will set us free". This is so true in my case. Unfortunately, regardless of Nick's deceit, all suffering was caused by Olivia's incorrect belief that I didn't care for her and my (possibly incorrect) fear that she might be trying to hurt me. Similarly, my fear of more pain was probably also ill founded or at least exaggerated.

I just needed to get a message out to Olivia and everyone else that was the truth. I just needed to say that I had merely been trying to tell another lady at the party that I didn't want to dance with her, because Olivia was there. I also needed to say that I had been badly hurt and that there was nothing I wanted more than to go out with Olivia again.

I probably only needed to say this to Bill and should have done so. Bill would then have conveyed this message to everyone else, the negativity would have stopped and the message would have got back to Olivia. However, I had had one layer of hurt heaped on top of another and I just did the man thing of going into my "cave". The more I got hurt the deeper I went into my "cave".

I had gone to the party still nursing a broken heart and was very nervous. The events of the party were very upsetting. Then there was the betrayal by a close friend, plus Olivia actually messing about with him. There was also the increased likelihood of losing Olivia completely. I also lost quite a few friends who ignored me, abandoned me, possibly encouraged a friend to pursue Olivia (at my expense), or were openly hostile towards me.

When was all this suffering going to end? Unfortunately, during these events, my mind had been full of hurt and fear. Fear is debilitating and caused me to react too slowly or incorrectly. Many opportunities were lost and it prevented me from resolving the issues that had arisen, especially when I felt badly hurt.

Fear is just False Emotion Appearing Real. It had created my reality which in 1979 was a living hell. Mind is the creator of the world you inhabit and is very powerful. The world we experience when we are asleep is similar to the world we experience when we are awake; they are all mere appearances to mind. Back in 1979 my mind of fear had created a living nightmare.

Problems arise when people become so emotional that reason is lost. There is simply no reason where strong emotions such as anger or fear prevail. Fear of more hurt had constantly prevented me from using reason and taking the correct and necessary actions, such as speaking the truth about my feelings.

The 2012 Tour de France winner Bradley Wiggins said "you have to keep your chimp in the cage - your chimp is your emotional side and in a pressure situation you have to react with logic, not emotion". A calm, peaceful mind is what is required. Reason and wisdom will arise when the mind is still.

Nowadays one of my golden rules is to never make an important decision while emotional. Many years later I would also learn about the benefits of meditation. Meditation is very powerful in providing clarity, while the mind identifies far less with any prevailing negativity and emotions. I find problems are always much smaller and the solutions clearer after meditation. This is similar to the way seemingly difficult solutions may suddenly appear during the stillness of sleep.

Concentration on something virtuous (or neutral such as the breath) provides mental stability and will result in inner peace. This can be found in the present moment, without being stuck in problems from the past or worrying about what probably won't occur in the future. Research shows that few, if any, of the outcomes of our perceived worries, ever come to fruition. Yet, as with me, so much negative energy is wasted when the mind is dwelling on problems from the past or imagined worries of what may occur in the future.

I continue to think that Olivia was and is perfect. However, I wish some of her actions at this time had been different. It is important to distinguish between a person and their actions. This is a bit like never telling a child he/she is bad or stupid, or he/she will identify with these comments, until he/she believes them, becomes them and they become a reality. In this way, the child isn't bad, it is the actions that are wrong.

I wish Olivia had given me a "lifeline" at that party. A simple smile would have been sufficient to allay all my fears. Unfortunately, Olivia made what appeared to be a desperate lunge for me. We were in the "gold fish bowl" of public scrutiny. It had all happened in an instant and actions taken and responses were influenced by fear.

I wish Olivia had not over reacted and had established the truth about my feelings for her before taking any action. However, most of all, I wish she hadn't started fooling around with a friend. That changed all the dynamics and (in my mind) created significantly more obstacles to a reconciliation.

Notwithstanding the above, I wouldn't criticise Olivia in any way. I'm sure she was also in a very low state and in need of friendship and company. I couldn't criticise her for handling matters badly, when I was totally inept myself. Indeed I didn't talk about the matter for many years, it was just too painful. I couldn't criticise her for poor communication, when I was abject myself. I certainly couldn't criticise her for still being crazy about me, for I felt the same way about her.

Having said how I wish Olivia had acted differently, I do totally accept that **I am responsible for all my own outcomes**. It is no use blaming anyone or anything else for what happened. If I hadn't been so hurt, and hadn't feared more hurt, I could have resolved all the issues with Olivia very easily. Indeed, regardless of the pain and fear, I should have found a way to speak to her.

Ordinarily, what I thought would happen, in a situation like that which occurred at the party, is that friends would pass messages to Olivia and me to help establish the truth and bring us together. However, soon I would only have a few friends left. From the dozen or so very close friends and dozens of other contacts and acquaintances I socialised with, I would soon count the number of remaining loyal friends on one hand.

Of all the friends who had bought me my prized Dunlop Maxply tennis racquet on my twenty-first birthday and the three close friends who a few months earlier had holidayed together with me, Bill was the only one I would see during the next year or so. When successful I had many friends, but once I had lost everything and was in a position of weakness, I inhabited a very lonely world. Whether it was merely perceived to be so or not, this nevertheless became my reality.

I'm sure Olivia would have let Nick down gently. I'm sure she would have told him that she valued him as a friend, but just as a friend and no more. At this point it would have been easy for Nick to say "you really want to go out with Paul again don't you?", "if so I can help it happen". Clearly this didn't happen and Nick was only concerned with self interest.

To this day I think Nick's actions were totally inexcusable. However, looking back, it is no use blaming Nick for what happened. He himself should have been of little consequence to the outcome. His actions should have been nothing more than a minor nuisance. Olivia was mine to lose. The real problems were purely in my mind, where their significance became greatly exaggerated. I now accept that the real enemy was my negative mind!

I don't want to say much more about Nick. I have expressed my views and feelings as they were. However, I don't want to get personal in any way. Where my views are incorrect I will say so and I do this later in the book. However, at this point I want my hurt and feelings to be clear to everyone.

Ps – at this point a friend who reviewed this book said she didn't think I was correct in saying I hadn't been personal about Nick

Consequently, I asked her to check that I had only been critical of his actions but not the person. Similarly, I have expressed my feelings, hurt and views at the time. Wherever, these views are not correct, I have tried to subsequently balance them later by stating the "correct view" in the light of Buddha's wisdom.

My friend subsequently re read the entire book and agreed I had done this.

1979 Dr Hook:
"When you're in Love with a Beautiful Woman"

Your teacher is always in front of you. During 1979 Dr Hook provided some great teachings on the nature of samsara. I use this Sanskrit word because there is no direct equivalent in English. For the purposes of this book samsara can be said to be the negative world that only brings suffering to an uncontrolled, negative mind and an uncontrolled, negative life.

If you have a negative mind, you will see and experience a negative world. It is only through learning to control the mind that you can learn how to experience inner peace and happiness whatever the circumstances. This samsaric life will always result in fluctuating between fleeting, temporary happiness and suffering. The prevailing state of mind will usually be hurt and suffering.

I think this is a beautiful song and was so appropriate to my situation. However, I wasn't yet ready to learn from these life lessons, until much later when I had access to some wisdom. Some extracts are below:

"When you're in Love with a Beautiful Woman"
- Wyilwabw - it's hard
- everyone wants her, everyone loves her, everyone wants to take your baby home
- Wyilwabw - you *watch your friends*...
- Wyilwabw - it never ends
- Wyilwabw - you go it alone
- maybe it's just an *ego problem*...
- everyone tempts her, everyone tells her, she's the most beautiful woman they know
- Wyilwabw - *you go it alone*
- Wyilwabw - *you watch your friends*...
- Wyilwabw - *it never ends*

I was being given some very profound, but painful lessons. Not only had I been given lessons on the nature of samsara, including my suffering, but I had also been given teachings on the impermanence of all phenomena. I had a very deep love for Olivia. However, we will all be parted from loved ones at some stage, even if only by death.

Also, by mixing a very deep love with a very strong attachment, suffering would be inevitable. These concepts will be discussed later in the book.

There is a story about a Buddhist Master Je Gampopa, who was grief stricken after the death of his beautiful wife. It was because of this death that he learnt about the lessons of suffering that came from attachment, death and impermanence. Death and impermanence being the very nature of samsara. This encouraged him to seek permanent liberation from samsara, which is characterised by suffering.

My circumstances were similar to those of Je Gampopa i.e. losing a beautiful partner. Maybe my situation was worse because I also had to cope with the loss of friends, hostility and (perceived) rejection. I had similar lessons to learn.

In the introduction I said that Olivia and I were "crazy" about each other. It is also common usage to say two people are "madly in love". Similarly, we say that "love is blind". Why is this?

Certainly my behaviour had been irrational and had led to disastrous results. All responses had been emotional and spontaneous. My actions were determined by fear, pride, hurt and attachment. Why should attachment cause these "mad" reactions?

Anger and attachment both derive from ignorance i.e. not understanding the way things really are. As such, they are like two sides of the same coin.

Anger is a response to a feeling of unhappiness, when people don't get what they want or get what they don't want. Anger results in people exaggerating the bad qualities of someone or something and a wish to harm her/him/it.

When under the influence of anger haven't we all done or said things we later regret? Hasn't anger at sometime made us all act in irrational ways? In this respect anger can be said to be "temporary madness".

Desirous attachment on the other hand results in exaggerating the good qualities of something or someone, desiring him/her/it and a wish to possess him/ her/it. Desirous attachment is characterised by uncontrolled desires or cravings (for oneself). Most of us mix love and attachment. Usually, the stronger the love is, so is the attachment.

True love is something pure and selfless that can never cause suffering. However, attachment is self-centred and will always result in suffering, as when we don't get what we desire or get what we don't desire.

I know my love for Olivia was very strong, but so was the attachment and this helped cause my "temporary madness", irrational behaviour, loss and suffering. I also believe that her exceptional good looks increased the attachment further. The uncontrolled desires also led me to mistakenly believe that she was a source of happiness for me. However, happiness is a state of mind and so its causes can only be found within the mind.

When I narrated the story to a friend and long standing client and showed him a picture of Olivia, he said "I'd have done something about it and spoken to her if I were you". It sounds so simple. He was of course right and I should have done so. However, the balance of my mind was disturbed.

I was suffering from the "temporary madness" of very strong attachment and debilitating fear. His advice was a bit like telling someone with suicidal thoughts "I wouldn't have wanted to kill myself if I were you" or telling an alcoholic "I wouldn't have had too much to drink if I were you".

Doesn't alcoholism (initially at least) derive from a strong attachment and uncontrolled desires, resulting from the mistaken belief that drinking is a cause of happiness and exaggerating its good qualities? The reality is that alcohol is a mind-altering, toxic, addictive drug, that can lead to depression, significant problems and great suffering. Even when taken in moderation, it only provides a "temporary reduction in suffering", a temporary escape from a (perceived) reality of a mundane, negative world and of worries, problems and anxiety.

My strong attachment with Olivia would keep me constantly thinking of the past, effectively mourning my loss or in the future dreaming of what might have been. This mind of attachment, whether in the past or future, just kept my mind in a world of misery. I needed to learn how to keep my mind in the present, where it could be calm, peaceful and relaxed.

I actually needed to concentrate on my deep love and not the strong attachment. I simply needed to focus on cherishing Olivia and not grasping for a result for myself. However, at this stage in my life I was living in ignorance, without even knowing that the main cause of my suffering was my self-grasping and my mind of attachment. The result was to live in a seemingly chaotic world, characterised by negativity, a mind in turmoil and great hurt.

Bodhisattva Shantideva says:

> *"All the suffering in the world comes from*
> *seeking pleasure for oneself.*
> *All the happiness in the world comes from*
> *seeking pleasure for others."*

Apart from "When you're in love with a beautiful woman", other big hits from 1979 seemed to reflect my situation. Amongst them were "We don't talk anymore" (Cliff Richard) and "Tragedy" (Bee Gees). Luckily, my sole focus was on "I will survive" (Gloria Gaynor).

3

Rock Bottom!
The Only Way is Up!

1979 was a very tough year. However, I was now determined to fight doggedly to turn my life around.

The first thing I did, as with any divorce, was to "carve up the territory" with Nick. The friendship was over and I didn't want any reminders of the most painful time of my life. Indeed the hurt was continuing unabated. I needed to move on, for my sanity as much as anything.

Ironically, directly and indirectly, I had introduced Nick to most of his social circle and girlfriends. I didn't hear from Ben or any of the Strollers football team, so that would become Nick's territory. I kept in touch with the girls from Pam's grammar school, started socialising more with my school sixth form buddy JB, started football training with JB's "Dynamo" team, often partied with Andy and his wide circle of friends and mixed with Bill and his friends.

Soon I would be socialising with my brothers' college friends and starting my new life at polytechnic. Job done, but it didn't reduce the pain!

Later in the year I decided to stop living a totally "ladish" lifestyle and to make my life a success, rather like a phoenix rising from the ashes. However, at the start of the year, I was still living a typical young man's life of beer, chasing the ladies and playing sport.

In many ways I lived a lifestyle that tried to block out the hurt and suffering. However, any relief was only temporary. I was later to learn that all these supposed "causes of happiness" were in fact only a temporary reduction in suffering and that if I over indulged in these "causes of happiness" then suffering would also follow.

This theory is called "**changing suffering**". For example if drinking alcohol, having sexual partners, eating good food or playing sport really was a cause of happiness, then the more I indulged the happier I should become. However, it didn't work and I still had an underlying suffering. I never had any more than a temporary reduction in suffering.

In the same way, if eating chocolate or good food was truly a cause of happiness the more you eat the happier you should become. Unfortunately, this is not the case. You can apply this to anything you enjoy. However, causes of suffering (like being poked in the eye) will only ever cause suffering and can never result in happiness.

Similarly, if we have too much of "worldly pleasures", such as eating, drinking, partying, then any happiness will turn to suffering. Conversely, having too much of a cause of suffering will never result in happiness.

I still needed to learn the lessons on the true causes of happiness and suffering and the conditions necessary for their creation. This was my most promiscuous year and there were lots of ladies. There was a lady I worked with, who later told staff she was pregnant with my child. There was a lady working as a maid on Jersey who took me back to her employers' house for a nude swim, while they were away. At the end of the year there was the very attractive Kate.

There were other ladies too, but none of them were Olivia. Having lots of ladies didn't make me happy. They just provided a temporary reduction in suffering. They were mere fleeting moments of pleasure, but the underlying hurt continued unabated.

Albert Einstein is attributed as saying "your greatest decision will be what universe you will live in". I had chosen a negative, hostile universe, which was determined by a negative and uncontrolled mind.

Despite my underlying suffering, there were many bright spots. In the summer of 1979, I had two great weeks on holiday on Jersey. I went with JB and some of the lads from his football team, with whom I had been training. JB didn't mix with the other circle of friends from school, nor did he know Olivia well. Consequently, he was unaffected by all the judgement, criticism and negativity that was following me around. JB was a good loyal friend and I got on well with his mates.

There were about six of us holidaying on Jersey and it was a typical lads' time involving sunbathing, drink, chasing the girls and playing pool. I remember becoming quite good at pool and beat a few other lads in the various pubs we frequented. Again I was reasonably good, but not exceptional. However, by really applying myself I could usually "punch above my weight".

Having apparently lost Olivia and a number of friends, I reasoned that I needed to start my life again. In September I decided to go to Huddersfield Polytechnic, as it was then called, to complete my accountancy exams. This would provide me with professional qualifications, a new home, new friends, a more exciting career and a student lifestyle with lots of drinks and parties.

However, life doesn't work like this and problems and challenges will constantly be thrown at you. Firstly, lots of ladies weren't making me happy, whilst drinking and partying just led to hangovers. Inevitably, this lifestyle just made me feel ill and tired.

At Huddersfield one of my first tasks was to organise a social life and make new friends, so I went along to the Polytechnic football team trials. I talked to a number of the players and it appeared that most of the team places would be taken with lads who played the previous year. There were probably only a couple of places up for grabs, but with the whole intake from new students I had many more skilful players in front of me.

My plan in the football trials was to get noticed by working harder than everyone else, constantly seeking the ball and using it wisely by always finding a better placed teammate with a simple pass. I needed effort to overcome my technical deficiencies. The plan worked and I was a first team substitute the following Saturday and a fixture in the second team for the remainder of the year.

The course proved to be harder work than I expected. It was scheduled to be completed in December 1980. There were four terms and three lots of professional exams, with about twelve papers in total. The exams in January and June were internal, but the finals were external, set by my professional body. It was intensive, the failure rate was high and the socialising often had to be sacrificed.

At this point I started becoming far less the party animal and became serious, studious and determined to succeed. I was now at a crossroads. Whatever I had done previously simply wasn't working. I certainly didn't know how to be happy and "**if you do what you've always done, you'll just get what you've always got**".

From this point onwards I started to plough all my energy and resources into my work and career.

Although I wanted to start life anew, in another area and to make new friends, it was tough. The problem was I couldn't rid myself of all the underlying hurt and suffering or forget about Olivia. Also, I now had to cope with massive change. On top of all the hurt, I had a change of job/workplace, a new temporary home, as well as being away from my family and my few remaining loyal friends.

When I started at college, I encountered my lowest point. It was in the first few weeks and I was very lonely. During this time, I frequently only had my thoughts for company, but they were negative and destructive. **The mind is a very good servant, but a very poor master** and mine was the latter.

I lived in a tiny bedsit and kept dwelling on the loss of Olivia and some friends. I remember sitting in bed, feeling all alone and having a solitary suicidal thought. This was the only such thought in my life, but it scared me. I was decisive and told myself to get this thought out of my head.

Although I didn't know it then, this was a profound moment. I had observed my mind. **Observing the mind is the first stage in controlling the mind**. The mind is very powerful and can be a major positive force or alternatively, if negative, can be very destructive. When you observe the mind, you are not identifying with the negativity. Consequently, I was not giving any power to the negativity and it quickly disappeared.

If we can observe and recognise fear when it arises, we can be separate from the fear and watch it drift away like a cloud in the sky. We can see it change and move on. The awareness that contains fear is never fearful itself. This concept can be applied to all areas of negativity, including perceived problems, anxiety and worry.

Soon after my brief flirtation with a suicidal thought, I phoned home and my mother told me a family friend Brian had just committed suicide. Brian was a few years younger than me and came from a Jewish background. I believe Brian had recently converted to Christianity and had clearly faced many dilemmas.

I was shocked and really felt for Brian. However, I had also received the wake-up call I needed. I knew I couldn't allow any more hurt to be heaped on top of the pain I was already suffering from. I simply couldn't continue to go through life in this manner.

How would I improve my life and ensure no more suffering? In my naivety, I devised a plan. I needed to make myself "confident and tough". However, when you are weak, vulnerable, sensitive, and have no confidence it's not easy. I would also come to rely on some of my greatest strengths i.e. being independent, determined, competitive, motivated and hard working.

It would be many years before I did gain access to the wisdom I needed. What I didn't realise was that I didn't actually need to gain anything, in reality I needed to learn to "let go". For example to gain confidence I needed to let go of all my self-limiting beliefs.

Similarly, to be strong and tough requires learning to "let go" of fear. With Olivia my problem had been fear of rejection and more hurt, especially after her fling with Nick. This had merely added to my fear of further pain. There was the possibility that she was so upset with me that she was trying to hurt me. I thought that love may have turned to hate. I just couldn't take the risk of any more suffering.

To quote Shakespeare's Caesar, "cowards die many times before their deaths; the valiant never taste of death but once". I had been cowardly in choosing the primeval "flight before fight", when faced with the opportunity to resolve matters with Olivia. I was certainly suffering and I reasoned I needed to achieve my objectives to become confident and tough (or fearless) to avoid any further catastrophes in my life.

❧

New Year's Eve 1979

I returned from college for the Christmas holidays and got in touch with Bill and the lads from the football team again. As soon as I arrived back in the Midlands I got in touch with Kate. She was a very attractive lady who had many male admirers and we started dating. Another leggy blonde with a great body, but she wasn't Olivia.

Just before Christmas I went to a party hosted by Pam's school friend Ellie. Less than two years previously Pam and I had helped bring about her going out with Nick for a few months. Ellie came up to me and said "why don't you see Nick anymore?". I'm sure the question was genuine, but I couldn't reply. To do so would have brought about a lot of painful memories.

Behind me, when Ellie asked me the question, were two friends from my junior school who burst into a knowing snigger. I don't know what story was circulating on "the street", but it was very hurtful. Maybe I was becoming paranoid, but I sensed I was the butt of many jokes. There were other scenes like this.

Looking back, the only thing that caused this pain was my negative mind of pride. People laughing at me does not, from its own side, cause any hurt. I can only suffer if my mind reacts in a negative way. I needed to learn the lessons of practising humility to dispel pride.

Buddhist master and Bodhisattva Shantideva says that "if someone calls you an ass, are you thereby transformed into an ass?". As the answer is no, why do we allow ourselves to ruin our own happiness? This is similar to Christ saying "turn the other cheek".

Similarly, Bodhisattva Langri Tangpa says in the sixth verse of the "Eight Verses for Training the Mind":

"If others out of jealousy or anger,
Harm me or insult me,
May I take defeat upon myself
And offer them the victory."

These were more lessons I needed to learn to lessen any future suffering.

On New Year's Eve 1979 Pip and Trish had another party. I guessed Olivia would be there and told Kate that I would be going to the party on my own.

As with the previous year Olivia turned up alone and again we were at opposite ends of the lounge. Bill then suggested that I should get drinks for him and a few friends, so I went to the kitchen on my own.

I wondered if Bill was trying to effect a meeting with Olivia. I went to the far end of the kitchen and started pouring the drinks. Within a few seconds Olivia was straight in after me. She seemed in a very determined mood and had obviously seen an opportunity to catch me on my own, away from public scrutiny.

As she entered the room she stayed close to the door (her escape route?), leaned against a wall and crossed her legs and arms. Her body language said that she was very defensive and was possibly prepared for a fight. My initial smile disappeared as I realised I may be in for a difficult and painful time.

Like a drowning man I needed to be thrown a lifeline. I just needed Olivia to do or say something positive. A smile would have probably been sufficient. I badly wanted to tell her the truth about the party the previous year and express my feelings for her. Unfortunately, her body language meant I was reluctant to leave my cave for fear of more hurt.

The events of the previous year and in particular her going out a few times with a former friend hung like a spectre over me. I did not and do not judge Olivia for her actions and I still wanted her badly. However, it hurt a great deal and had introduced the notion in my mind that Olivia may have wanted to hurt me and seek some sort of revenge. The fear of further pain meant I would hand the initiative for any reconciliation to Olivia. Unfortunately, I simply wasn't taking responsibility for the outcomes in my life, particularly with Olivia.

Sadly, neither of us was prepared to say what we really wanted or to express our feelings. The discussion just involved small talk asking about how each others' family were and about me going to college and her career.

She did appear to throw me one cryptic lifeline. She said that going to college and qualifying as an accountant was presumably the most important thing in my life "wasn't it?". I had another opportunity to express the truth. I should have said "no you are the one thing I desire most". Unfortunately, the initial emotional response was to fear getting hurt further. So after a pause, I just meekly nodded in apparent agreement, while waiting for her to say something positive that would give me cause for encouragement.

Then Bill came into the kitchen. I'm sure he was playing the role of a concerned and loyal friend and had come in to see if I was ok and if I needed any more help. Soon Olivia left the room in a very purposeful manner, without explanation and almost in mid sentence. I'm sure she was doing to me what she thought I had done to her at the party the previous year.

Another opportunity was lost. Bill turned to me and said "are you ok?". Out of male pride I nodded yes, but I wasn't. I felt like a fighter who was on the ropes and had taken yet another blow in a savage beating. Fighters in that situation will invariably try to soldier on and try kidding themselves and others that they are ok. Mind and pride can play all sorts of tricks and convince you of anything. Maybe it's a survival strategy, but it didn't help.

All along I was picking up mixed messages from Olivia. It was now clear she still had very strong feelings for me. However, were they positive or negative? Had love turned to hate? Did she want reconciliation or revenge? I wasn't going to take any chances that would leave me at risk.

There was only one thing I wanted more than Olivia and that was avoiding any further hurt. At least that was always my initial emotional response.

After returning to the party Bill chatted to his wife Farida (aka "Fred"), a friend also called Paul (aka "Nesha") and Nesha's wife Jacqui. I'm sure Bill had reported the conversation in the kitchen and very kindly Jacqui then presented me with the greatest opportunity of all. She hurried over to me and rather impatiently said "look, do you want to go out with Olivia, because if you do, we can arrange it?".

Jacqui must have heard the word on "the street", that no one had relayed to me, that Olivia still wanted to go out with me. Great, all I had to do was to say yes.

Although I had been thrown a lifeline, it was all a bit too quick and she required an immediate answer. I needed to be handled very delicately. I still felt like the fighter on the ropes, barely conscious and taking one punch after another. After being hurt again, I simply wasn't in a position to think straight and my proud mind also got in the way. I just meekly nodded no. Again instinctively my emotional reaction was "flight".

Within seconds I realised my mistake and turned to talk to Jacqui to tell her the whole story. It was too late, Jacqui had returned to the others and was in deep conversation with a group of people. I had just missed the best possible opportunity. My remaining friends would have fixed things for me.

Looking back on what happened reminds me of the film "Sliding Doors". I had a number of opportunities to rectify matters with Olivia and each time an instantaneous "flight" response made me make the wrong decision. Each such moment was truly monumental and resulted in massive changes to our lives. We could have been together again for the long term. However, my decision making had been catastrophically poor.

My pride, not to show my vulnerable side or any sign of apparent weakness, would again cause further and unnecessary suffering. The reality is the reverse. Showing your vulnerable side is more a sign of strength than weakness. However, I wasn't going to tell others how hurt I was, especially as some were being hostile towards me. Pride would never let me admit I was hurt and/or beaten.

"**Pride always comes before a fall**". Pride (when exaggerated and/or incorrect/deluded) is another negative and destructive mind that needs to be controlled. My pride meant I was pretending I was ok and it also meant I wasn't being truthful about what I wanted or what my true feelings were. Pride just prolonged the problems and made them worse. My pride also meant Olivia would not learn how deeply I truly felt about her.

Years later, I would learn what makes a person strong and it's certainly not living a proud life of deceit (by not being open). To be strong, live a problem free life and to be able to sleep at night, thoughts, words and deeds need to be in harmony, starting with a pure intention in the mind. Our mental actions need to be free of ego, which causes division, fear and insecurity, creates negativity and only looks to satisfy our own desires. Our intentions need to be to help others. More lessons to learn!

I looked for Olivia. I wanted to pluck up the courage to talk to her again. But would she reject me again, as I felt had occurred in the kitchen? It was too late. She had left the party well before midnight, probably also hurt and disappointed.

Looking back, it seems to me that we were both acting in a similar way. I believe we were both fearing rejection and further hurt. Also, we were both too proud to show our vulnerable side, admit to each other that we had been hurt and that we still wanted each other (badly). For both of us, **pride and fear** would prevent us getting back together. Certainly, these minds were my greatest enemy.

On numerous occasions, I had been hampered by a proud mind. Was Olivia also now doing the same? I wondered if she had been advised to treat me badly or hurt me, as people (mistakenly) believed I had done to her. Certainly the results were disastrous for both of us and pride was a prominent contributory factor. My untamed pride was a greater enemy than any person could be.

The only other thing I can then remember was Bill grabbing me from behind to start a conga. I think he was loyally trying to do something to shake me out of my melancholia and perk me up.

There were no other New Year Eve parties and I didn't have the opportunity to meet and talk to Olivia again for some years. I often wondered if the first party was arranged to enable us to get back together and whether Olivia wanted the second party to have one last go or to make her response statement to me.

I was constantly picking up mixed messages from Olivia. Before the first party I didn't know whether or not Olivia still had strong feelings for me. The upset at the end of that party indicated that she did. However, fooling around with Nick suggested that those strong feelings may now be negative and that she may be trying to hurt me.

Similarly, the dramatic and quick entrance to join me in the kitchen at the second party reinforced the notion that strong feelings must still exist. However, as with fooling around with Nick had, the dramatic exit, without any explanation, could be interpreted as "sod you, now I'm going off on my own and I don't care if it hurts you".

These mixed messages were an indication of the poor communication between us and I simply had had too much hurt to enable me to risk any more pain or rejection. Fear would still rule and dictate my actions. I fully accept that I could have corrected the misunderstanding at the first party and should have done so.

This mess was entirely of my own making and I didn't or couldn't rectify things. The reality was, I had no one to blame except myself.

On reflection, I believe Olivia and I had been so badly hurt that we couldn't act rationally and needed help. We needed positive friends who would establish that we both had strong feelings for one another and wanted to go out with each other again, more than anything else. I needed friends who would act as a go-between, as Jacqui had offered to do. It was clear; we were out of control and couldn't resolve the situation. We simply couldn't do it on our own.

Our problems were being played out in the public arena. We had created our own soap opera and most of our "friends" chose to hinder rather than help. Their default setting was negativity. We needed help, but our public predicament seemed to bring out the worst in most people. Many chose to judge, criticise, gossip maliciously, covet, be aggressive/hostile etc. Their actions just caused a greater obstruction.

The innocent victims who would suffer from the above actions were Olivia and myself. We needed to be able to **observe "the play" rather than to participate in it**. However, this was extremely difficult to two people so young, naïve and hurt.

The play cast Olivia as the poor innocent victim and me as the uncaring villain. The reality was that the real villains were the negative states of mind of various people, resulting in all the harmful actions. I include my own actions, although these were not intended to hurt anyone. They were merely, but mistakenly, trying to protect myself from further suffering. Nick's covetous intent was inevitably particularly damaging.

I had Bill and a small number of other friends who remained loyal. Unfortunately, the positive and loyal friends, acquaintances and contacts seemed to be heavily outnumbered by the negatives ones, who I felt I couldn't approach for help. At least that's the way it seemed to be. I believed some friends were probably encouraging Nick to take advantage of Olivia's mistaken belief that I didn't care for her. Otherwise, he probably wouldn't have taken the risk of losing all his friends.

Looking back, at the very least, I know I should have confided in Bill and asked him to help. I should have told him that I was badly hurt and couldn't take any more pain, that I had merely been trying to politely tell another lady at the first party that I didn't want to dance with her, that I still wanted Olivia more than anything else and that I badly needed to end all the madness. Regrettably, I didn't. I was too proud and I would live to regret it.

The way I had acted reminds me a bit of Danny (played by John Travolta) in the play and film Grease. He had met the beautiful Sandy (played by Olivia Newton-John) in the summer, but when she turns up at his school he is caught between admitting his love for her and acting "cool" to his friends. My motivation in acting the way I did was to deny and not let anyone see my hurt and vulnerability. However, male pride hindered both Danny and me.

Why won't men open up and admit their vulnerability easily? We seem to be conditioned from an early age not to admit that we are hurt, presumably in case it is perceived to be a sign of weakness. From an early age we are told that "big boys don't cry". Consequently, when we are in a bad way and genuinely need help, we don't ask for it. I needed help and couldn't resolve the issues on my own.

I tried to act with dignity at all times. I didn't criticise anyone, even Nick. However, I was only giving off the wrong messages. It probably appeared to everyone that I didn't care about Olivia or the current predicament. I simply took one blow after another squarely on the jaw. My (male) pride also prevented me from admitting any weakness to anyone who I felt had wronged me, abandoned me or was acting aggressively towards me. The messages I was giving off weren't mixed, they were simply wrong.

To progress in life I would need to learn to be **open**, as well as honest and would also need to learn how to practise **humility** to be able to dispel my pride. I would need to have the humility to admit mistakes and weaknesses and to show vulnerability where it existed. Most importantly, I would need to learn to take **responsibility for all the outcomes in my life**. Unfortunately, these lessons would only be learnt much later in life.

This was my lowest point, but in the words of the song "the only way is up". So began my personal journey of development and discovery, but it wasn't easy. I was starting from a low point and was young, naïve, inexperienced and lacking confidence.

I also had to face the fact that I was a loser! It's not easy for a proud mind to accept this. It's usually easier to blame others. However, you can't develop and improve until you know your faults and weaknesses.

Clearly Olivia still had strong feelings for me and she was the most important thing in my life. I had a beautiful lady and a lovely (but hurt and fragile) person, who was as crazy about me, as I was about her. I had everything on a plate and I had blown it all through fear, pride and naivety (ignorance).

I was a loser!

I wondered many times how I could rectify the situation. I thought about writing to her to explain the truth. It would have been so easy. However, fear always stopped me. I had been hurt too much and badly lacked confidence.

Yes, I was a loser and I needed to learn how to succeed in life and avoid any such pain ever occurring again.

It was the primeval "fight or flight". With Olivia I had mistakenly chosen "flight". In the rest of my life I needed to learn the lessons and make sure I could always succeed and overcome fear.

Certainly in my case, and I think for Olivia too, the fear of rejection, based on mistaken appearance to mind (jumping to incorrect conclusions and beliefs), had become a self-fulfilling prophecy. The fear of rejection had led to it actually occurring. False imaginings in mind had led to our unwanted reality, the worst case scenario.

The world was perfect but my negative mind had led to great loss. It was only years later that I was to learn that "**there are no problems outside the mind**". Learning to control my mind, so as to always achieve a positive outcome was to become a big learning lesson.

Maybe suffering would turn out to be a gift.

In 1998 a young David Beckham playing in a World Cup match against Argentina petulantly kicked out at an opponent, who made the most of the situation and Beckham was sent off. England fought hard and played brilliantly with ten men, before losing after extra time on penalties. The next day Tony Blair, the then Prime Minister, talked about ten heroes and one stupid boy.

Beckham was vilified by what must have seemed to be the whole nation. Opposing fans jeered and booed his every touch in the 1998-99 Premiership season. In the first away league game of that season, at West Ham, a Beckham effigy was seen dangling from a hangman's noose. The Manchester United's team coach was pelted with stones and beer glasses as fans vented their frustration, chanting "We hate Beckham" and "You let your country down".

Beckham has recently admitted "I have nightmares about France 98", he also said "It will always be with me" and "It was humiliating". He went on to be England captain, have a great career, became a much respected ambassador for his country and a superb role-model for young boys aspiring to be footballers. Beckham became England's most capped outfield player. Through a determined, positive attitude his lowest point became a springboard for his success.

Would Beckham have been so successful without this early adversity? Could I now use my greatest trauma in a similar way as an opportunity to be successful, lead a meaningful life and find happiness? Would my suffering turn out to be a gift?

With all adversity there are said to be two darts hitting you (the target). The first dart is the incident itself, in this case constantly feeling rejected and missing opportunities to have what I really wanted. The second dart is how the mind reacts and this is usually the cause of greatest hurt. In this respect pain is inevitable, but the suffering is optional. Unfortunately, I had no knowledge of how to turn a negative mind into a positive one. This was to be my greatest lesson.

It was only many years later that I would learn how to control the mind, what are the true causes of happiness and suffering and how to maintain a calm, peaceful, relaxed mind regardless of the darts that life throws at me. Even with the theory, being constantly vigilant of movements in the mind and becoming familiar with and applying effort to my practices would be necessary.

If happiness and suffering are states of mind, then their causes can't be found outside of mind. Mind is so powerful and is the creator of your world. This means you can have control over all outcomes, whether positive or negative. You just need to know how to do it. That is where wisdom comes in.

I must stress that I have never blamed or judged Olivia for any actions. I don't think I've ever said a negative thing about her and I certainly never will in the future. Both then and now I have only had positive thoughts of fondness, respect and love towards her. I am happy to accept that the poor outcome and the hurt and suffering I have endured are entirely my own fault.

I would frequently think fondly of Olivia and what might have been, but there was also often a lot of hurt and suffering. I often found myself singing the David Bowie song "Sorrow". The chorus was "with your long blonde hair and eyes of blue, the only thing I ever got from you was sorrow". This was of course incorrect, the relationship had involved many great moments, but when my mind was negative it just seemed to be true.

Regardless of what I thought when negative, I do consider Olivia to be perfect. I now take **responsibility** for all my outcomes and any problems should have been resolved by me. This shift in my mind from one of fear, blame, excuses and denial to one of a totally positive attitude, owning, being accountable for and being responsible for all my outcomes was to become a major and fundamental change for the good. Now, whenever problems occur, I always ask myself "how can I turn this into a positive opportunity?" and there is always a way.

Now to get on with the rest of my life, but would there ever be a reconciliation with Olivia?

Is your world illusion or reality?

For my "O" level English Literature I studied Wuthering Heights and enjoyed the book very much.

At the time, I thought it was a love story. However, I now realise it was more about attachment and uncontrolled desires. Like most of us Catherine and Heathcliff mixed love and attachment and so it becomes a story about love, loss and suffering. Pure love is selfless and never causes suffering. It is the attachment and uncontrolled desires that are selfish (or self centred) and cause the suffering. I will explain this more fully later.

Briefly, for these purposes (desirous) attachment can be said to be exaggerating the good qualities of something or somebody, thinking it is a cause of happiness, desiring it and wishing to possess it. As such attachment is a delusion in mind and is not pure as love is. The element of attachment is looking for a result for ourselves, often to the exclusion of the object or other person. Attachment is therefore based on desire for our own happiness, frequently without consideration for others.

There were parallels in "Wuthering Heights" with Olivia and myself. A central part of the story is when Heathcliff overhears Catherine talking to her housekeeper Ellen about him. Ellen asks what she plans to do with Heathcliff and if she is likely to marry him. Catherine says there is no way she would consider marrying Heathcliff because of his lack of status and education and she wishes to marry another.

107

Catherine says,

> *"It would degrade me to marry Heathcliff now;*
> *so he shall never know how I love him: and that,*
> *not because he's handsome, Nelly, but because he's*
> *more myself than I am. Whatever our souls are*
> *made of, his and mine are the same; My great*
> *miseries in this world have been Heathcliff's*
> *miseries, and I watched and felt each from the*
> *beginning: my great thought in living is himself."*

> *"If all else perished, and he remained, I should*
> *still continue to be; and if all else remained, and*
> *he were annihilated, the universe would turn to a*
> *mighty stranger: I should not seem a part of it.*
> *My love for Linton is like the foliage in the*
> *woods: time will change it, I'm well aware, as*
> *winter changes the trees. My love for Heathcliff*
> *resembles the eternal rocks beneath: a source of*
> *little visible delight, but necessary. Nelly, I am*
> *Heathcliff! He's always, always in my mind: not*
> *as a pleasure, any more than I am always a*
> *pleasure to myself, but as my own being."*

Heathcliff only hears the first (negative) part of what Catherine says to Nelly, is distraught and leaves to go to America and make his fortune. Unfortunately, after he leaves Catherine expresses her great love for him.

If Heathcliff had heard the full conversation he would possibly have been able to develop the relationship and much suffering could have been avoided.

When Heathcliff returns Catherine is married, has a daughter and things can't return to how they were or how they could have been. Basically, through misunderstanding the situation, opportunities would be lost and their lives would never be the same again.

The key thing here is that what is in mind is illusory. Mind is the creator of our world, based on our experiences and perceptions and it is a different world for everyone. Clearly Catherine and Heathcliff didn't communicate their feelings for one another very well at all. Heathcliff's belief about Catherine's love for him, was largely based on the experience of half a conversation and Catherine's state of mind at a particular moment in time. Consequently, this premise was incorrect.

Similarly, Olivia seemed to have built up a belief that I didn't care for her when nothing could have been further from the truth (as had Heathcliff with Catherine). I also had uncertainty over whether or not Olivia wanted me or was intent on hurting me. I now believe all these doubts were unfounded.

In Buddhist terms "mistaken appearances" to mind ("ignorance", not "truth"), or an "illusory" mind are the ultimate cause of all our suffering. This is a major lesson to be learnt.

There is a famous eight verse narrative, by Geshe (Buddhist Master) Langri Tangpa. The final verse of the "Eight Verses for Training the Mind" refers to this. The relevant part is below:

> *"...with a mind... that sees all phenomena as illusory, may I be released from the bondage of mistaken appearance and conception."*

It is very liberating when you can accept this and even more so when you can actually let go of the negativity, created by the ego and the mind that cherishes oneself. This mind views everything from the reference point of oneself and leads to us exaggerating our self importance. The inevitable result is suffering.

✌

The Turnaround (the 1980s)

I was told later in life that "what makes a man strong is when, starting with a pure intention, thoughts, words and deeds are in harmony". These are the actions of mind, speech and body. Previously, with Olivia, I'd been thinking one thing (how hurt I was and how I longed for her), saying nothing (retreating into my cave when hurt) and acting differently, as though I was ok (giving the impression I didn't care).

Ego just always gets in the way. No wonder I messed things up. It would be much later that I finally made a "declaration of truth" and utilised its power. Would this be too late?

I had effectively been living a lie and had clearly given the wrong messages to Olivia. If we live a pure, truthful life in harmony with the environment (without looking for a result for ourselves), everything works out fine. Intentions need to be pure and all actions of body, speech and mind need to be in harmony.

I find this wisdom about truth everywhere and this includes openness as well as honesty. Being "economical with the truth" also doesn't work. Simply avoiding lies, means actions of thoughts and speech are inconsistent. It is always worth considering the words of Desiderata, "Speak your truth quietly and clearly; and listen to others, even the dull and ignorant; they too have their story". What a pity we don't have sufficient (access to) wisdom when we are young.

Youth really is wasted on the young. However, we need to learn from our experiences, mistakes and failures. Similarly, suffering can be useful and I was reappraising my life to ensure I wouldn't be a loser again. I needed to learn that I was responsible for all my outcomes and could affect them all positively.

I spent 1980 at Huddersfield Polytechnic and the summer on Jersey, with JB, on a working holiday.

I still wanted Olivia badly. I was caught between escaping to start a new life, in the naïve hope that everything would then work out perfectly, while I still hoped to bump into her again and to work things out.

Hope is not a good strategy for anything. In business I tell all my clients not to rely on hope, but to make sure they plan and control their businesses. Hope was certainly not a good strategy for meeting Olivia again and indeed it would be a long time before I would get to meet her.

Nowadays, in my life, unlike in business, I try to practise patient acceptance. This is very different from trying to control your world. As soon as we have desires and want the external world to be a certain way we will be disappointed. We all want different things from life and the world simply isn't going to be the way everyone wants it.

Bodhisattva Shantideva says "if you want to protect your feet, would you cover the whole world in leather?". In the same way, it is easier to control the mind than to constantly try to change the world to make us happy. Unfortunately, I still had this massive lesson to learn.

If you can live in harmony with the world and the environment you live in, without trying to control it, things will usually work out fine. I have learned from experience and know this to be true from some of the amazing events that have occurred through the practices of patient acceptance and letting go, rather than controlling (or looking for a result).

By this time, I was working and studying hard. I had learnt lessons previously from trying to hold my place in the football team. Football was the sport I loved most, but it wasn't the sport I was best at. I was frequently one of the least gifted players in the squad and had little pace.

I learnt that to retain my place in the football team I would need to work harder than the other players, constantly look for the ball and not give possession away cheaply. It was the same at school; I was in the top class of my grammar school, but near the bottom of that class. I really didn't bother at school, but now I would.

It was the same when I started squash, golf, racquetball and tennis. I was able to win minor trophies at all these sports, but I was always well behind the county players. I reached a similar level at all these sports. In squash I was the equal of a good Warwickshire or Worcestershire ladies county second team player. I could play for the teams in a poor club or in the bottom men's team at my club, but I was well behind the best men.

So I knew that if I wanted to succeed I would need to work harder than many of my peers. I did this and passed the professional exams with reasonable grades in January and June 1980. Now I was ready for the finals.

The finals were intensive. I returned to college in the September and we had to sit the papers in mid December. It was a tall order, as the failure rate was high. However, I reckoned that even if I failed, at least I would get to a reasonable standard. I passed two of the papers, but failed two narrowly (within five per cent of the pass mark).

The following June I sat all the four papers again. This time I passed three papers and failed the one narrowly. This meant I only had to re sit the one paper in December 1981. I passed this and was admitted to membership as a Chartered Certified Accountant in early 1982. I had done it! I was now a qualified accountant. I had climbed the mountain that qualification represented.

In general these times were still very tough due to my negative mind. The mind is like Velcro when it comes to negativity. Negativity just sticks, causing constant problems unless we are vigilant. Similarly, the mind is like Teflon when it comes to positivity. I needed to learn how to turn negativity into positivity, because the events of 1979 were constantly holding me back.

It was my competitive instincts that had pulled me through my darkest period. I simply wasn't willing to give in and I fought my way out of my predicament.

I had fulfilled my part of the contracts offered by life. At school, in the top class, we were constantly told that we, the intellectual elite, would be running the country in the future. I believed this to be relevant to the brighter lads. However, I too should be able to find a privileged role in life. There was always the assumption that having a good education and passing exams would lead to a good job and a happy life.

I'd had a good education and was now a qualified accountant, but it took me years to get over it. The education system simply didn't prepare me for life's problems. You're simply not told how to be happy, deal with problems and be free from suffering. Our education system seems to be based on the false premise that education, qualifications, good jobs, high salaries and material possessions are causes of happiness.

Basically, after school you're thrown into the deep end of the swimming pool of life and need to teach yourself very quickly how to swim through the currents of worries, stress and problems.

Similarly, I'd fallen in love with a beautiful lady, but I certainly wasn't living happily ever after. I needed to learn how to be happy and free from suffering. Only years later would I learn how to maintain a calm and peaceful mind; how happiness can only be attained if you have inner peace and how to be free from problems. At this stage in my life I certainly didn't have inner peace.

I continued to work hard and arranged my life so as to have plenty of excitement. However, my mind simply fluctuated between excitement and despondency, rather like a balloon in the wind, depending entirely upon external circumstances. Continually, I would find that Velcro in my mind would ensure I couldn't forget the events surrounding my loss of Olivia and the perceived betrayal by friends and the complications this caused.

The hurt and suffering would return and continue for some time. Pain seemed to be the "default setting" in my mind.

During the summer of 1980 I did have a break from college and work. I spent this time on Jersey with my school friend JB. Although I would have low points thinking about the loss of Olivia, there were many good times. This was the time of the Moscow Olympics, the ensuing mass boycott, Daley Thompson, plus the great Seb Coe and Steve Ovett rivalry. On balance it was a very good working holiday.

After college I ploughed all my efforts into work and my career. I rented a house with my brother Cab and one of his friends. I also joined a small firm of accountants, while continuing to study to re-sit the final part of my accountancy exams.

Through working so hard, I was learning an important lesson. By concentrating on something else, I was not focusing on the negativity that caused my problems and suffering. **Concentration provides mental stabilisation**, but without it the mind is weak.

On reflection most of the 1980s were devoted to hard work and my career. There was less time for girlfriends and to be honest I wasn't ready for any serious relationship.

The events of 1979 had left some scars. I needed to protect myself from ever getting hurt so badly again. After events like this it is common to build protective layers around oneself and I certainly did that. My drawbridge came up and my portcullis came down.

In 1982 after qualifying, I got a job working as a Company Secretary and Accountant for the local subsidiary of a large plc, which was a stockist and supplier of welding rods. This was my first management position. It was tough and demanding. The accountancy qualification provides an excellent technical training. However, it doesn't provide much training in managing people, which proved to be the hardest part of the job. The technical side was easy.

I did find this and subsequent management roles in the 1980s very stressful. The combination of this hard work, the stress involved and the emotional scars meant I wouldn't be ready for a serious relationship for some years. Anyway, Olivia was a very tough act to follow.

The role for the large plc provided an excellent training in best practice for large company financial control. At the same time my father was involved as non-executive chairman of a privately owned protective clothing and safety equipment company. My father recognised that this job would provide ideal experience for being able to control the family business.

In 1982 I bought my own house. It was in the same road where Cab and I were renting a property. Again, I was fulfilling my part of life's contract. But the assumption that money and material possessions lead to happiness is flawed. I was finding this out from personal experience.

Money, material possessions or looking for, desiring or attaining anything in the external world does not lead to happiness in itself. I had desired qualifications, money, good jobs, beautiful women and status, but still couldn't find happiness. If I didn't attain what I desired then I would be unhappy. Unfortunately, when I did attain what I desired, as I was doing throughout the 1980s, more desires would simply arise.

If I had a good car then I would want a better one. It was the same with jobs, salary, holidays and property. I was beginning to search for the real purpose in life. I was beginning to realise that all conventional roads to success and happiness were deceptive. Years later I would learn of the importance of cultivating inner peace and practising contentment. However, I still needed access to wisdom.

The Great American Adventure (1981)

I had a great adventure in September 1981, which provided a much needed break from work and my career. Andy organised a car tour of the West coast of America. Our tour included San Francisco, Los Angeles and San Diego, through the Nevada desert to Las Vegas and back via Yosemite Park.

When Andy first mentioned it he had about seventeen male friends interested. However, by the time of the trip and the various girlfriends and partners had had their say, there were just the three of us Andy, John and myself.

John was in a similar position to me, in that he had married my childhood neighbour Bev, but they had recently separated. John was always very successful with the ladies and had had a number of very attractive girlfriends. This holiday was no exception. John was the most successful with the ladies.

We drove about 3,000 miles in a hire car and had quite an adventure taking in all the tourist sites like Hollywood, MGM studios, the Disney theme park, the Las Vegas casinos and nightclubs etc.

John has always been very fit and sporty, so we would spend the days jogging, playing racquetball, on the beaches or by a pool and sunbathing. Andy on the other hand preferred the electric, vibrating beds in the hotels, "cruising" the many tv channels (we only had three or four in Britain then) and visiting science museums. Andy used to say that he loved the many adverts on American tv, but he thought the programmes ruined them.

By the end of the three week holiday, John asked me if I was interested in starting a new life afresh in America. I think we were both keen to escape from our past relationship problems and the idea of starting a new life, free from the past, sounded very appealing. However, my experience at Polytechnic had taught me that the location didn't really matter; it wasn't easy to escape from the mental anguish that the mind creates.

It was really my negative mind that I needed to escape from. Also, I felt I needed to stay in Britain to complete my accountancy studies and gain my qualification. Moving abroad, at this stage in my life, was a step too far.

We had one memorable experience in San Diego. This was southern California the land of hot sunny weather, lovely beaches, surfing and beautiful girls. John and I wanted to spend the day on the beach. Predictably, Andy said he would rather visit the science museum. Having checked out of our hotel earlier that day, we mistakenly left Andy with all our belongings, in the boot of the car. John and I had little more on us than trunks, flip flops, towels and a few dollars in change. We didn't even have any clothes with us.

We arranged to meet Andy early in the evening, at the corner of a "block", which I marked on a map. John and I had a great day and then tried to find Andy at the arranged place, but he wasn't there. We scoured the area, but there was no sign of him, so we had little choice but to wait by the beach where he had dropped us off.

As dusk fell it started to get cold. We had little money left and more importantly the atmosphere was changing. The happy tourists were long gone and had been replaced by dodgy looking locals. We clearly looked like tourists and many of the locals looked like drug dealers, addicts or petty criminals. The atmosphere was now very intimidating.

John and I had left our credit cards with Andy and we spent most of our remaining money on the phone. Unfortunately, the nearest British embassy was in Los Angeles and they were very unhelpful. By about 10 pm there was still no sign of Andy and we were now getting worried. Finally, as a last resort, we phoned the police.

Soon afterwards a police car did appear and the officer was brilliant. He confirmed the area was dangerous at that time and offered to drive us around and look for Andy. Firstly he took us to a local hotel and told the manager that if we couldn't find Andy, he would personally guarantee our bill. What an incredibly kind gesture for two foreigners.

The officer then took us on a drive to find Andy. We were now safe and warm, and had the security of a hotel bed to fall back on. This drive turned out to be quite an adventure. Soon after getting into the car the officer received a call notifying him of a probable mugging and shots being heard in a nearby park. We gave chase, with John and I two frightened onlookers in the back. It was just like a car chase in an American film, but this time it was for real.

We didn't catch any criminals and thankfully we weren't fired at, but nor did we find Andy. The police officer took us back to his station and I think it was about 11 pm. Finally we were safe and the tables had been turned. We were all now more concerned about Andy than about ourselves. Then a message came. Andy had finally phoned the police station. The officer dived across the desks, hurriedly picked up the phone and shouted "Andy, Andy where are you?".

Andy was safe, but hadn't been able to read the map properly and had been waiting all along about a mile from the correct "block/corner". We were soon reunited and we had yet another great "Andy story" to tell everyone back home.

Massive Goals

I ran three marathons in 1983, 1984 and 1985. The first was in Sandwell and the last two were in Wolverhampton. I did this with Geoff from the Stompers football team. He just told me three months before the actual event and said he was entering with four of his brothers, who all played for the same team. Having five brothers entering the same marathon was quite unusual and they were pictured in the local papers.

I had always wanted to enter a marathon and jumped at the chance. It was a big challenge. Geoff and I went straight out for a two mile run and I felt awful. I thought, if I'm struggling to run two miles, how will I possibly manage to run 26.2 miles with just three months training? However, the body can be very powerful and can be trained to perform outstanding feats very quickly, especially if the mind is positive.

Geoff's brother Richard gave me a copy of a running programme, from a specialist athletic magazine, recommending a plan to get ready for a marathon in three months. Brilliant, this was exactly what I needed. Each day there would be different exercises and distances, building up to a long run at the weekend. Some days there would be short bursts, other days it would be hill running and sometimes it would be slower, but longer runs. The long distance run each weekend would increase progressively, until two weeks before the event there was a twenty mile run.

I stuck fairly closely to the programme, whatever the weather. The other lads from the football team were better footballers than me and were faster. I ran some of the longer practice distances a few times with Geoff. To begin with Geoff would always run ahead, laughing because I couldn't keep up. However, I always overtook him a few miles later as he started to tire. I just kept plugging away and always finished strongly. His excuses became legendary.

Like everything else, I found myself to be quite good at long distance running. I wasn't brilliant, but I was reasonable. However, my biggest strengths were my single minded determination and competitiveness. When it came to the big day of the first marathon I finished in a very creditable three hours and thirty-five minutes, just outside the top twenty-five per cent of participants.

I have a great picture of myself and Richard crossing the finishing line together, holding hands with arms raised. We finished well ahead of the other four brothers. Having run the first marathon in three hours thirty-five minutes I then set myself a target for the second marathon the following year. The target was to average less than eight minutes per mile.

My plan for the second race was to run the first seven or eight miles at a gentle jog in eight minutes per mile. Then I would run the next twelve miles or so fast (for me) at an average of seven minutes per mile. From the twenty mile mark, as the body tired, I just needed to average ten minutes per mile to achieve my target.

I ran the race almost exactly as I had planned and even shaved a couple of minutes off the target, to finish in three hours and twenty-seven minutes. I think I was inside the top twenty-five per cent of the runners. Again I was learning some important lessons. With hard work, sheer determination and will power, I could outperform people who had more ability.

In three years I had qualified as an accountant, run two marathons in good times and was progressing well in my career. In 1979 I had been a "loser", with no self confidence and a mind of fear. I had then lost the most important thing in my life (Olivia). That would not happen again and I was learning about the power of my mind and how to become successful and a "winner".

Looking back the only criticism of my marathon times was that I set such a very modest target for improvement in the second race. It was only eight minutes quicker. Later in life I would learn about the **power of my mind** and about **setting massive goals**, I would adopt the belief that "**if I aim for the stars, then even if I fail I will reach the moon**".

If I had set a target of three hours for my second marathon, I'm sure I could have beaten three hours fifteen (or even ten) minutes. If I had beaten the target of three hours, then I could have then set another target for the next race e.g. two hours forty-five minutes.

The third marathon was actually the one I got most satisfaction from. I had been under pressure at work and had not trained so hard as with the previous races. Consequently, my body just ran out of energy too soon and I really struggled. I "hit the wall" early and came in with a time over four hours. With the second marathon I had been very fit and it was always just a question of how fast I would finish. This time I was in real danger of not finishing at all. Again, my single-minded determination pulled me through.

I will always value these marathons and the lessons they taught me. By simply throwing myself in the deep end and facing all my fears, I could achieve virtually whatever I wanted to. I could eradicate all those debilitating fears and overcome any self limiting beliefs. The former world boxing champion Mohammed Ali is attributed as saying something like "**what the mind can conceive, the body can achieve**". This was quite a transitional period for me.

∽

A New Career Move

In mid 1983 I joined my father in the family business. The company was a distributor of protective clothing and safety equipment. I had had ideal experience with the stockists of welding rods and now had experience of big company financial controls.

My father had considerable experience in business, having successfully founded and grown a number of companies in the past. He was now chairman of the family business, but, in his words, was a "sleeping partner". He was a very good leader and strategist and we formed a good combination, with me taking the lead in all financial matters.

I had always said that I wouldn't join the family business until and when I had proven myself elsewhere. With my accountancy qualification and experience I was now, if anything, over qualified for a business of this size. I had heard that it was far more difficult working for your father than working elsewhere or for anyone else.

Again the difficulty is one of perception (illusion in the mind). Working elsewhere I would be perceived as an experienced and well qualified accountant. Working in the family business I would frequently be perceived as the boss's privileged and undeserving son. This would occur where employees who might have been with the company for many years, but had little or no professional qualifications, would feel over-looked or even, in some cases, jealous.

Although the technical aspects of financial control were simple, I was still inexperienced in managing people and this would create difficulties for me. The family also had a minority shareholding, which would make it difficult to effect any change that was necessary. Managers and other shareholders would often fight against the changes necessary to implement financial controls and to restore the company to profitability.

The company also had difficulties, was poorly controlled and needed someone like me, but wasn't big enough to attract anyone of sufficient calibre otherwise. When I joined the company the exact financial position was not known. Financial control was so poor that there was virtually no up to date or accurate management information.

My father didn't know how bad the actual financial predicament was. If he had the decision may have been taken to close the company. The company was losing money heavily, up to its overdraft limit, under pressure from the bank and was in the thick of a significant recession. Also, the other shareholders were not experienced in operating at this level.

Although my family only had a minority shareholding, it was my father's reputation and personal guarantees that were keeping the company going. Nevertheless, the bank must have been very close to calling in the receiver.

There was no time to ease myself into the job. I had to swim quickly or the company would almost certainly drown. Within three months the cash control had improved significantly and we had accurate monthly management accounts, with full comparisons against a robust budget. No management can make effective decisions without good information. We now had this and the cash, tight because of heavy losses, was at least much better controlled. Customers were paying quicker, bad debts were reduced and suppliers' terms had been renegotiated to ease the pressure on cash.

The position was very difficult. There was a culture of poor financial control and management would frequently fight against the changes necessary for improved fiscal systems. It was here that I was to learn how damaging ego and pride could be. I came to the conclusion that people would often be overly concerned with reputation, position and status. The conclusion I came to regarding those I worked with, was that they would rather be perceived to be the main person in a small and poor organisation than the second in charge of a large and successful organisation, even though the latter would provide greater financial reward.

At the end of the day, people will act out of self interest, unless you can convince them that their interests are your interests and unless you can get people to "buy in" to work towards the same goals. Also, there needs to be a professional control culture, whereby people know they must adhere to tight financial systems.

A poor control culture is difficult to change and those who are inefficient and/or looking to perpetrate fraud, will always argue that controls, tighter systems and management monitoring are not necessary and will never work. It frequently happened in our company.

We needed to save the company and effect change quickly. Unfortunately, other managers and shareholders either didn't have the will or ability to improve matters. They merely needed to co-operate with us, but would usually fight change rather than be seen to be compliant with new much needed corporate policies. Our minority shareholding made effecting change very difficult.

Management monitoring is also a vital aspect of running a company. **"Management should inspect and not expect"**. Basically, **"what can't be measured can't be controlled"** (e.g. costs and margins). Without monitoring procedures, standards will invariably fall. We had the situation where salesmen were selling at very low margins and people wanted easy access to expenses, without any authorisation. Also, overheads were running well above (primitive) forecasts.

When I arrived forty percent of the sales were to the then British Leyland. Everyone in the company jumped whenever they called and margins were ridiculously low. If you were to apply the Pareto principle then we probably got eighty per cent of our hassle from companies providing twenty per cent of the profits. Things needed to improve, but effecting change would not be easy.

Restoring the company to profitability was a bit like turning a battleship around. Initially, it is a very slow process, but once you have turned it around, you can then gain momentum and speed. With accurate information we quickly managed to make the necessary changes to get the company to a break even situation. Slow progress was then made in the next two years to make modest profits.

By 1985, we were ready to gain speed and momentum.

A new Female Companion

In every walk of life I had always had very close friends. Unfortunately, things were different now. I had been hurt so badly that I wouldn't let any lady close to me. I had built a lot of barriers around myself in order to protect me from getting hurt again. Unfortunately, I would also be so protective as to not allow love in.

It was similar with male friends. Through every stage of my life I had always had very close companions, but not now. It would be some years before I would be able to trust anyone again. I was like a wounded animal and for a few years I would even push away my long standing remaining close friends. I became more of a loner.

Much later, a client told me about his wife leaving him for another man he knew in their social circle. The client said "after something like that you never trust anyone again". I can relate to that and I was in a similar position. I just ploughed all my efforts into work and material success.

Then in April 1984 I did gain a new companion who gave me unconditional love. Her name was Fatima and she was born in the horse riding stables, just over the road from where my parents lived. One of Fatima's parents was a Bavarian sheep dog. Fatima looked just like that parent and had very distinctive colourings. Her body was predominantly white with a few large black patches. She had one black ear and her head and face were predominantly ginger. She was gorgeous and with her distinctive markings everyone in the neighbourhood came to know and love her.

Fatima had two brothers "Winston" and "Churchill", who remained at the stables. Both looked just as Fatima did, like Bavarian Sheep dogs. One was ginger and one was black. Both had a few white patches.

Fatima was so named because she liked her food so much. The owners just assumed she would become fat. Although smaller than Winston and Churchill, she would always be the first to the food bowl and was fully prepared to let them know that she intended to eat before them.

My first memory of Fatima was when, as a puppy, Cab brought her to our house for a trial run and to get her used to her new home and owners. Cab had to drag her the last hundred yards, while she had a "sit-in" style protest. It looked funny to see her being dragged slowly on her backside to her new home.

Fatima soon adapted to her new environment and we converted an old shed for her to sleep in. Her brothers visited us soon after her move. My father says she proudly took them on a tour of the garden and to see her home. It's interesting to see the strong territorial instincts develop. Fatima often went across to the stables, would walk into their house and eat her brothers' food. However, her brothers could play with her in our garden, but were not allowed into our house and would certainly never be allowed to share her food bowl.

Often when my father took Fatima around the lanes for a walk he would be joined by her parents and brothers. Her family were welcome to walk with us. However, none of them were allowed to be stroked by my father or me. She was fiercely protective of us and her status.

Fatima was a great character with her own distinctive personality and there are many fond memories of her. One day my father told her they were going to Clent for a walk over the local hills and she dutifully got into her seat in the back of the car. Then as they left the drive Winston and Churchill turned into it looking for Fatima. My father let the brothers into the front of the car, so that they could also go on the walk. Unfortunately, Fatima objected to them having the best seat and fought with her brothers all the way to Clent.

There are other great Fatima stories. I remember Cab arriving at my parents once for Sunday lunch. Fatima came bounding up to Cab and as usual made a real fuss of him. Cab said "hello Fatty", not knowing that the lady next door was behind the hedge. She replied "hello". Cab came in to lunch laughing uncontrollably.

She was my father's dog and Fatima used to love the daily walks. However, I was an equal favourite, because I would let her off her lead, so that she could romp and explore at her leisure.

As a puppy Fatima was full of beans. My mother tells of how Fatima terrified some repair men in the lounge as she barked from the hall. She took a run up, then jumped feet first, about four feet high, through the swing doors, looking like a flying Superdog. The repair men hid terrified until she was ushered out.

One day I took Fatima for a walk along the lanes and at the bottom of the drive stopped to put her lead on her. Unfortunately, she got so excited she started jumping up me and had a freak accident. She trod on the clip of the lead, so that the sharp rigid section was digging into the bottom of the fleshy soft part of her paw. She tried to break free, but each time she landed the metal would dig into her paw and she squealed continually in obvious pain.

As Fatima frantically moved around squealing she looked me in the eye for help. As I grabbed the lead she stopped jumping and yelping. Unfortunately, in order to release her, I had to squeeze the clip, putting more pressure on the tender paw. She simply trusted me implicitly to act in her best interests and free her from pain. She allowed me to increase her pain for the few seconds that were necessary, in order for me to eventually free her. This event seemed to increase the strength of our bond.

Fatima used to enjoy a mock fight with me, so I got an elbow length leather gauntlet from the family business. As soon as I put the gauntlet on she would go wild with delight and playfully attack me. Even in play and with the gauntlet for protection, her teeth were sharp and her jaws powerful.

One day I fell asleep after Sunday lunch on the settee. My father watched Fatima jump on the top of the other end of the sofa and walk along it, like a tight rope walker. She then leapt on top of me for a playful "fight". I woke with a shock to see my father almost wetting himself with laughter.

Fatima loved her romps over Clent Hills and didn't want to return. She would get very excited at words like "walk" and "Clent", start barking frantically and run as fast as she was able around the house. I soon learned that if she didn't want to return home, I needed to carry on to the car, otherwise she would play a game of running off every time I approached her. However, she knew how to lead my father on and he never got the hang of her games.

One day my father turned up late for a meeting with the bank manager to discuss the financing of the family business. He was in a very agitated state. He rushed off straight after the meeting because Fatima was still at Clent. He need not have worried, she was sitting there waiting in the same spot where my father had parked his car. Fatima must have been there waiting patiently for about two hours.

Only once did Fatima get the better of me with her games. I took her to Malvern for a walk with JB. JB and I had a few pints of beer and then took her for a walk in a woodland area of muddy banks and streams. Then the heavens opened and it poured with rain. JB and I wanted to return but Fatima didn't. To chase her would have meant running and probably falling down the muddy banks.

We gave up and slept in the car until she returned a couple of hours later, looking like a drowned rat. She was filthy and wet and made a real mess of the car. However, I couldn't get mad with her; she had enjoyed herself so much.

At Christmas 1989 I returned home after six months working in Canada. I phoned and told my father when I was starting my drive back from Heathrow. In turn my father said to Fatima "Paul's coming back". She waited dutifully by the lounge window, looking up the drive, for the whole of the four hours or so it took me to return home.

After my father died in 1992 Fatima would spend hours out until late, presumably looking for him. Fatima became a great companion for me. We developed a great bond and understanding. Whenever, I was at a loose end and needed companionship over the weekend, I would go and take Fatima for a long walk over Clent Hills. This was a great comfort to me as I rebuilt my life, dealt with the pressures of work and looked for a new partner.

Fatima would teach me about **trust and unconditional love**. The bond between man and dog is special. Fatima provided great company and trusted me implicitly. Providing they are treated well dogs keep their part of the contract with their owners. It is invariably humans who treat their dogs badly, rather than the other way around.

The Gambia

Early in the spring of 1985 my father suggested going on a holiday together to The Gambia. We had both had a tough time trying to save the family business and it seemed like a great idea. The pressure and stress at work had taken its toll on me and I felt I needed a break. These days I had fewer close friends and I was ploughing too much effort into work. The hurt from the split with Olivia, the circumstances after the split and the subsequent loss of friends had also left its mark. This was also the period when I had few girlfriends. Consequently, I had few distractions from a life of hard work, worry and stress.

The holiday was very enjoyable, but I made one big mistake. The week long holiday followed my marathon and I asked the doctor if I could have the necessary inoculations immediately after the marathon and just before the holiday. This was later than was usually advised, so as not to take any risks that might affect my health during my marathon performance.

Unfortunately, the body is quite run down after a marathon and I became quite ill after the inoculations. I developed the worst cough I had ever had and I passed it on to my father. Dad had also been a heavy smoker and had already had heart trouble, so it affected him badly. The extremely high temperatures also made us feel worse.

This one and only trip to Africa was a real eye opener. We did all the usual tourist things and stayed in a great hotel. We also tried to take in the local culture. We visited schools, the local markets, local villages, a zoo for tourists and had a boat trip on the river.

We would usually be greeted by happy smiling local people. School children would run up to us with big broad grins, their white teeth gleaming in vivid contrast to their dark skin. They would be delighted just to be given biros. Similarly, the adults in markets would be happy and friendly. There would also be a far more leisurely and relaxed atmosphere. I can remember a taxi driver stopping to have a chat with his wife and later stopping at shops, en route to taking us to our destination. The whole pace of life was slower and in deep contrast to my own lifestyle and the culture I was used to in Britain.

My greatest memory and lesson from this holiday was that people living in conditions, that we in Britain would consider to be extremely poor, appeared to be happier than in the wealthy country that I lived in. I surmised that, providing people weren't in danger of famine, starvation, war or disease, they could be happier without the wealth and material possessions that we strive for in Britain and the wealthy countries.

My mother often says "**possessions bind**" and I was starting to learn this from my own experience. Whatever you acquire can also be the cause of problems and suffering and I was learning that constantly striving for material goods doesn't bring happiness. Similarly, satisfying desires just leads to more desires, rather than happiness.

For example having wealth can lead to worries about the value of properties, shares and other investments, people coveting what you have and distrust for financial advisers, accountants and solicitors etc. Similarly, having a car will lead to large bills for services and repairs, break downs, accidents, difficult insurance claims, people scratching it maliciously etc.

Our holiday in The Gambia was very enjoyable and taught me a lot about the priorities in my own life. It raised questions about whether or not the material goals prevalent in our society are correct. I still believe that goals such as financial security are important. However, they should not be the only objectives in life. Ideally financial security should merely provide a platform for a meaningful life, helping your community and others. This trip also increased my questioning about the real causes of, and conditions necessary for, happiness.

On this vacation I read two books; "Conspiracy" about the assassination of President John F Kennedy and a book by Jeffrey Archer called "Shall we tell the President", again about an assassination attempt. When we left The Gambia there was increased security and intensive bag searching. Apparently, the President of the country was on our flight. I was asked to leave the plane and go back for a second search and interview with the security staff. I'm sure it was because of the books about assassinating presidents.

It was an amusing end to an excellent and valuable trip.

Andy, the Health and Fitness Freak?

Andy's priorities at this stage were still socialising, electronic gadgets, science and organising discos with Tim and other friends. Consequently, my parents came back one day shocked that they had seen him walking the Clent Hills. This appeared to be completely out of character. Had Andy now decided to get fit or was he starting to enjoy nature and exercise? Had he turned over a new leaf?

I gave him a ring, as I was intrigued. I needn't have concerned myself that he might be trying to get fit and healthy. He told me he had been walking over the hills to test his new transmitter from the highest point in the Midlands.

Panic over, Andy fully intended to stay unfit! I promised him I wouldn't tell anyone I'd seen him walking over the hills, just in case they got the wrong idea. It wouldn't have done his reputation any good at all.

Grandad – the End of a Great Innings!

Later in 1985 my Nan died at the age of eighty-nine. Her health had been declining and her heart simply stopped working.

Nanny and Grandad had been physically in good condition for their age. This was partly the result of teaching dancing until they were well into their seventies. Although she was physically very fit, sadly my Nan suffered from dementia in her later years. One day she came up to Grandad and me in the kitchen of her house and said "Bert, please can we go home". Typically Grandad dealt with this issue with humour. It was his way of coping with with problems. He would simply crack a joke.

Poor Nanny just looked confused. She simply didn't recognise her home. It was sad to see her suffer like this, but at least she had a good family around her.

Grandad's ability to laugh at adversity was an inspiration to us all. His faith also helped him and in his later years he attended church services most Sundays. He was also very good at practising contentment. He didn't wish for much and was happy with his life, provided he could go to the Baggies (WBA FC) matches and socialise on his frequent walks.

The rest of the time he would watch snooker, cricket, tennis, football and most sports on his television.

In 1986 Grandad celebrated his ninetieth birthday. We arranged for him to meet the Baggies players in the dressing room before the home match. Grandad loved it, but the Baggies were now in the (old) second division and were to languish in a state of mediocrity until 2002, when they finally got promoted back to the top division. Some of the football in this period was very poor and we really suffered, but I was really hooked and it was as though my blood was blue and white.

At the age of ninety Grandad was still very fit and he still enjoyed his daily walks chatting to all the neighbours and shopkeepers, but he would spend most time talking to the ones who were Albion (Baggies) fans. He was a great character and everyone loved him. My mother and her sister Aunt Enid tried to persuade Grandad not to go to the matches anymore, because of his age. Quite rightly he argued that he really enjoyed the football. Indeed it was now the most important thing in his life and so I continued to take him to all the matches.

Then at one Baggies match in 1988 I went to the toilet at half time and stopped for a chat with my friend Tim, who still accompanies me to all the home matches. Grandad had said he was ok and wouldn't need to move. When I got back to my seat he was being helped by two St Johns ambulance men, who were trying to get him to drink tea. Unfortunately, Grandad had decided to stretch his legs and had fallen down some concrete steps.

I asked Grandad why he didn't drink the tea and he replied he didn't want to catch AIDs, which was the big scare at that time and he hadn't grasped what it was about, or what the causes were. He must have been the only ninety year old concerned about catching AIDS. Unfortunately, the fall down the steps did affect Grandad badly and his arthritis became much worse. This caused him pain and affected his ability to walk.

1987 provided another landmark in my life. I stopped drinking. To begin with I simply wanted to lose a bit of weight. I then started to reason that it was good not to frequently wake up with a hangover. In our society drinking is mistakenly regarded as an integral ingredient for being happy. Fortunately, I was beginning to realise that it just provided a temporary reduction in suffering, an illusory escape from a world of difficulties.

I was starting to become very health conscious and it was apparent that drinking the amount I did would only lead to long term health problems. I regarded myself as a social drinker, but I was lucky enough not to develop any addiction problems. Drinking a few pints with "the lads" had become a way of life. Also, being competitive, I couldn't rest unless I drank as much as all the others.

We live in an odd (macho) society where we almost have to apologise for not wanting to put into our bodies toxic, addictive, mind altering chemicals, that make us feel ill. Fortunately, I was highly independent and very much "my own man". I would no longer be influenced by peer pressure and I decided not to drink to excess again. I have been virtually teetotal ever since. Grandad, talking about pubs, always used to say "the best side is the outside". He was right and I finally took his advice.

Wedding Bells at Last

I was now the manager of the Stompers second team and both Pete and Cab played in it. Pete was captain and my brothers were probably the best players. They could probably have both played for the first team, but I think they preferred to play with and for me. Cab was always hampered by his asthma. He would always start the season well, but struggled with his health once the bad weather started.

In the summer of 1986 my brother Pete married Kay. The best man dropped out just before the event, so I did the job again. This time I was still nervous, but a lot more confident than when I did the same job for Gaz.

I organised the stag night, which involved drinking lots of beer at the local pubs. I woke up the next morning with a bad head and a blond in my bed. Unfortunately, it was just Pete.

My speech went down well. I said that as his football manager I had tried Pete in every position, but I hoped Kay had more luck. I said I'd just be saying a few words "off the cuff" and then pulled off a false shirt sleeve with my speech written on it. Grandad certainly enjoyed the speech and jokes.

The following Christmas Eve Kay gave birth to my lovely, sweet niece Danielle. Dana as she called herself has lit up the family and is always incredibly smart, attractive and pleasant. I tell everyone that she got the Webb looks, but unfortunately I didn't.

Pete, now an economics graduate, also worked in the family business, learning his trade as a sales representative, before taking on senior sales roles with a larger company.

The Family Business

By 1986 the family business was now making acceptable profits. My father had also recognised that we could sell the same products, from the same Asian suppliers, into other markets. For example we had expertise in buying industrial safety gloves and these could be sold into the gardening centres and DIY "sheds".

I had now been the Finance Director in a small family business for a number of years and longed for career progression, either in a larger company or in a different role. Consequently, I headed up the new division and was also responsible for selling to the "sheds" and handling the other new accounts that had been acquired in our new business. These accounts were large and the customers were household names.

This new role did provide me with a fresh challenge. I also went to college and studied at night to gain a marketing diploma, which was relevant to my job and would help me in my new career. Undertaking a "sales" role would also provide new challenges. Although I was gaining in confidence, I would still not have seen myself as a salesman. However, I now had the opportunity to gain additional skills and develop myself further.

I had moderate success with selling and gained two new large gardening contracts with "sheds" that were household names. The future of the company now looked much brighter and we now had a solid financial base and modest profitability to build on. Unfortunately, the management team was still inexperienced. The future of the company was also totally dependent on my father's leadership skills, his strategic awareness and my financial control.

Unfortunately, in my father's state of health, the stress of trying to save the family business and deal with the politics of shareholders and managers fighting change and their machinations in manipulating staff to improve their status, had taken its toll. He had also become very disillusioned with the self interest and poor values prevailing in business and he really wished to retire.

My father and I talked about the continuity of management. I was now experienced in financial control and was learning about selling, marketing and strategic planning. However, I was still inexperienced in management and believed that my appointment as Managing Director would be met by resistance from another manager who was older and coveted the position. This manager was not a shareholder and had no professional qualifications, no knowledge of financial control, no planning capability nor any marketing skills.

This manager's experience was limited to operational skills such as product knowledge, distribution and selling, which are just three functions of the overall marketing mix. We could have worked well together and our skills complemented each other's. Despite this, I knew he would only be happy if he had the main role, even if he didn't have the necessary skills. I knew he would make life very difficult for me if I was the MD and the other managers were not strong enough or experienced enough to help in any period of transition involving massive management change.

We had a choice, either to appoint me as the Managing Director, working for my father as the non-executive Chairman, or to sell the company. By 1987 I had now had over seven very difficult years. This time had been dominated by the devastating loss of Olivia, betrayal and abandonment by friends, pushing myself and working very hard to gain good professional qualifications, holding responsible management positions with various companies, saving the family business from insolvency, fighting management, boardroom politics and the machinations of other managers and shareholders.

The role of Managing Director would have been an interesting challenge. However, there would inevitably be more hassle and difficulties, before things would get better. The stress of the last few years had driven me to be relatively successful, but had not made me happy. I now took the view that there were more important things in life than status, reputation, money and material possessions. I needed some time off from the emotional roller coaster that I had been on, to plan and enjoy the rest of my life.

We took the decision to sell the business and my father put the feelers out amongst his business contacts. My father was determined that we wouldn't just sell to the highest bidder, but that we would find a good home for the company, to ensure its future prosperity and to look after the staff.

After a few months my father had found a buyer. It was a local plc with a very good reputation. They made an offer which was acceptable. It wasn't brilliant and things could be done to reduce our capital gains tax liability. Unfortunately, my father confided in me that his health was so poor that we had to sell quickly, without wasting any time, even if it meant not getting the best possible deal. There was no option but to agree.

Within a few months the due diligence process was completed. I would soon be free to start a more meaningful career and life, or so I thought. Frustratingly, the buying company's professional advisors said that I was an integral part of the continuity of our business and that I was necessary to ensure the plans were met and to formulate future strategy.

This was bad news for me and meant we could only sell the family business if I signed a three year contract and committed to being the Managing Director. My father's health and the family's finances required that I signed this contract. It meant my "escape" to pursue other interests would now be on hold for three more years.

Worse still, if I did sign the contract, I reasoned I was in for three more very tough years. There would be pressure from the plc on me to deliver the financial returns they wanted and there would be pressure internally to lead the inexperienced management team, including the one who coveted the MD's role for himself and would constantly be difficult and cause problems.

The job of MD was a "poisoned chalice". Unfortunately, I had little option but to sign the contract for the sake of my father and our family. I had to put my own wishes and ambitions on hold for at least three years, as I always kept my word and honoured every contract I signed.

My mindset was such that I expected difficulties and sure enough they came, virtually as soon as my appointment was announced. However, looking back maybe I brought these problems upon myself. I really needed to observe the "play" rather than be in it. If you identify with your negative thoughts you just give power to them.

It is how the mind reacts that determines whether you have a problem or an opportunity or challenge. Back then I still saw too many problems. This was purely the reaction of a negative mind. I was gaining in experience and confidence. Despite this, I still had much to learn about controlling my mind.

Shortly after we sold the business the purchaser was itself bought by another plc. Our new masters were run by two young whiz kids. There were immediate management changes and the original group Finance Director was "put out to grass" and appointed Group Secretary. He now had an administrative and legal role. The new young Group Finance Director was young, brash, aggressive and racist.

My father and I went to a number of meetings involving the two young Chief Executives and their Group Finance Director. We were not impressed by their values or their bravado. We had tried our best to find a good home for the family business but, through no fault of our own, we didn't trust the new owners to provide continuity or integrity.

Part of the price we would receive for the sale of the company was to be determined by future profits and it wasn't long before the new Group Finance Director would try to manipulate our profits to reduce our future payments. I decided I couldn't work for these people, but if I chose to leave it would mean I would have less influence on the future profitability of the business and our future receipts.

Finally, I made the decision to leave at the end of 1987. It was in unpleasant circumstances, with one internal manager being as disruptive as he possibly could. My previous Managing Director (of the welding rods company) often said, in his down to earth black country accent, "**I usually find it's them what shout loudest about the boat sinking, what am rocking it**". How true this would always prove to be.

Again, it's a case of "**uneasy lies the head that wears the crown**". This was yet another example that if you have reputation, position, wealth or a beautiful partner then others will desire and covet them. Others will almost stoop to any lengths to acquire what you have and that is simply the way it is. They will support you in so far as you are in a strong position. If your position weakens then they will plot and make their move.

The negativity spread, as it always does and after I went to speak to the Group Operations Director, to express my wish to be released from my contract, he withdrew all support for me. Legally, I needed to be released and made it clear I hadn't resigned. However, the group officers tried to claim I had resigned and tried to avoid making any further payments due under my contract.

I was not trying to profit from the situation. Consequently, I negotiated a settlement of just three months money. Their actions were vindication of my wish to leave. Soon afterwards the new group was declared insolvent. I believe one or both of the two Chief Executives fled and were investigated by the Serious Fraud Squad. I also believe the actions of the Group Finance Director were investigated by the authorities and/or the Institute of Chartered Accountants in England and Wales (ICAEW).

It was a sad way to finish my work in the family business after implementing the big company financial controls that had made a major contribution to saving the company and providing an excellent platform for future growth and prosperity. I would rather have left entirely on my terms and with appreciation from everyone for my contribution. However, that was just my personal wish and the self interest of others would and always does prevail.

I would later read an article in The Independent, dated 2nd December 1997, saying that the former chairman of the group had stolen thirteen million pounds and had received a six year jail sentence. The group had net debts of more than one hundred million pounds.

This final liquidation in 1997 was described as "the curtain being drawn on one of the most complicated and controversial corporate disasters ever known".

Again my wish to leave was vindicated, as I couldn't work for unethical employers.

My father and I had to negotiate for a remaining sum in lieu of our "earnout" contractual entitlement, or the payment we should have been entitled to for future profits. Although there were some very difficult times in the family business, the experience of turning it around, dealing with difficult, selfish managers and the exposure to dishonest group officers would provide me with excellent career experience.

Indeed I now regard myself as a good judge of human character. Subsequent experience in fraud investigations would improve this "bloodhound" instinct for detecting dishonesty.

When I left the business, my father explained the situation to my brother Pete. He said it was he (my father) and I that had saved the company and that no one else was involved. He meant that everyone else performed purely an operational, not a strategic role and was in particular referring to those managers who were very negative and acting out of self-interest. They were just "runners", who would carry out my father's directions.

After I left, the family business continued to progress for about six months. Well run companies should be able to operate without the main directors in the short term. The inexperienced remaining management took the credit for the good results. However, without an effective strategic input and planning capability, companies will fail in the medium and/or long term. Six months after I left, the company started to decline rapidly. My father used to say "**success has many fathers, but failure is a bastard**". How true this has proved to be throughout my business career!

I liken people in business to the population in Britain during the World Cup. Every man drinking beer in every pub thinks they can do better than the national manager. So it is with employees and managers, they usually believe they can all do better than the directors. The reality is usually very different, as it was with our business.

After we sold the business and I left my father told me that if he had his time again he wouldn't go into business with anyone except me, he then added "or family". I'm sure he was confining his remarks to me and my brothers. After a distinguished career, although constantly being let down by people he had trusted, my father was very disillusioned with human nature and the ethics and values prevalent in business.

During his career my father had held the belief that if people are surrounded by honest, hard working colleagues they will rise to match their peers. Unfortunately, his experience had been that negativity was more likely to triumph. Honest and hard working people would tend to fall to the level of the weakest and most negative; he would often say **"the chain is only as strong as the weakest link"**.

In 1988 my father suggested a number of business ideas for us to pursue together. I considered them and then told my father that it was probably best if I went my own way in business and in life. This was no reflection on my father, it was purely that I wanted to stand or fall depending entirely on my own efforts. If I worked for, or with my father, the perception of others would always be that I was a favoured son, who hadn't achieved anything on my own merit. I now needed to succeed entirely as a result of my own efforts. Failure was no longer an option.

My previous boss had always told me that working for your father was twice as hard, due to the mistaken perception of others. I thought that being a qualified accountant would correct this perception, but it didn't.

Now to open a new chapter in my life and to put those dark days behind me.

4

The Light at the end of the Dark Tunnel (1988 to 1994)

1988 marked the end of my dark period. We sold the family business, which had been the cause of much stress and hassle. I completed my marketing diploma, which would improve my business ambitions and found a temporary job as an accountant with a large plc. This enabled me to relax more and spend more time playing squash, which was to become my main sport and pastime for quite a few years.

While working in this temporary role I met Sally. Sally was a very pretty girl of twenty-two, who was studying to become an accountant. The company we worked for had just taken over a smaller group in the north of England and we frequently travelled up there together in my car.

Sally and I soon started dating. This was my first serious girlfriend for ten years, since Pam and Olivia. I simply hadn't been ready for one before then. During that time, I had been channelling all my energies into taking exams, my career and business. I had become very serious and had been affected by the stress of management roles, saving the family business and the daily pressure of helping to run businesses. Also, I still hadn't properly got over Olivia and all the trauma following our last meetings.

I had had a few years where I had been too serious and anxious. I hadn't been the same happy go lucky person I was during the good times. I simply wasn't in the right frame of mind to attract a positive lady. Basically, **I had taken myself** and my perceived problems **far too seriously**.

With less work, pressure and hassle, I was now able to enjoy my leisure time much more. Sally was exactly what I needed. She was taking professional accountancy exams herself and so would be happy for me to pursue other interests such as squash and football.

Sally is black. Her mother was from Jamaica and her father had an interesting background of being part black, with some Puerto Rican and Jewish ancestors. This resulted in Sally having a quite distinctive and very attractive look. She was a very caring and genuine person, who I have the greatest respect for.

I remember once meeting a businessman who started talking in a racist way. I just looked at him and said "actually my girlfriend is a black, Puerto Rican, Jew". He looked at me not knowing if I was joking or not, but at least he stopped talking in such an offensive manner. A colleague then leant over and said to him, in a show of support (to me), "Paul doesn't like racism". The point was made without any aggression on my part.

Sally would often look after her nephew Leroy, who was four years old when she and I started going out. Leroy never knew his father when he was young. He was a lovely lad who enjoyed my company. Spending time with me enabled him to do all the things he should have been doing with his father. I was with Sally until 1994 and would frequently take Leroy to football matches, or to play squash or tennis.

I remember the first day I met him, little Leroy wanted to give me a picture of a dinosaur he had just drawn. It was very touching. Why should an incident like this remain in my memory? This selfless act of **giving and cherishing others** provided genuine happiness and fond memories.

On the other hand, while I had been continually striving to fulfil my own personal ambitions and desires, I had been pursuing selfish acts that had only led to more unhappiness, stress and pressure. **Pursuing personal desires merely leads to unhappiness** if we don't get what we want. On the other hand if we do satisfy a desire, there will always be another one to replace it.

We had a good time with Leroy, who would often prefer to go to the football with Cab and myself, to staying with Sally. Once, at a football match, a young Leroy asked me "what happens if, when they kick the ball in the air, it hits a bird?". It's interesting how the minds of young people work.

Once I took Leroy to a match where the referee was very poor. Leroy turned to me and said "Paul, this referee is so bad, even the fans are singing the referee is a w**k*r". I just said "yes, he is very bad, but please don't repeat that to your mother, otherwise she might not want you to come to the matches with me".

I lost touch with Leroy shortly after I stopped going out with Sally, but I often wonder what happened to him. I'm sure he will have grown into a fine young man. His mother and Sally were very strict with him, but this ensured he grew into an honest and trustworthy teenager. I remember being told that for the first few years of life a child just needs unconditional love. After that a child then needs discipline. I'm sure Leroy will prove to be evidence that this is true.

In August 1988 I got a permanent job with a large company specialising in metal and plastic stockholding and distribution. I was now an employee and consequently didn't feel as though I had as much stress or pressure. Indeed after all the hassle, machinations and politics of the family business, where we never had a majority shareholding, I could now relax and enjoy life.

Between my first and second interview the plc I joined had been taken over by a larger plc. However, I reasoned that this would provide greater opportunities. Anyway, I was now determined to be in "relax mode". I would be with this group for over nine years, by far my longest period of employment

I was now seriously considering what is the true meaning of life. If I analysed my life then it was apparent that opportunity, qualifications, hard work, better jobs, striving for more money, reputation, position and better material possessions had not provided me with happiness or freedom from problems. I was now starting to move from ambition to purpose.

In 1989 Grandad died at the age of ninety-three. He was prepared for his death and would often say "I've had a good innings and now I'm ready to meet my maker". I last saw him in hospital a few days before he died. His body was now deteriorating rapidly and I remember Sally, who had worked in a hospital, had to help him onto a commode. Grandad just smiled at me and said "you too can have a body like mine!", a line from the companies selling body building equipment.

This comment was typical of Grandad. Even on his death bed he was cracking jokes and making fun of his predicament, which was imminent death. He was well loved and was missed by the whole family. He taught me **humility** and **contentment**.

Canada

In early summer 1989 my employer asked if I would like to work in Canada for a while. The VP (Vice President) Finance was a lady from Hong Kong, who was pregnant and wanted to

148

take a few months off, before and after the birth, to be with her baby. The head office was based in Toronto and there were branches in Mississauga (West Toronto), Calgary and Montreal.

I had created a good impression with my boss the Divisional FD and it sounded like too good an opportunity to be true. It sounded very exciting and it was. Toronto is near Niagara Falls; hosts the Blue Jays baseball team; isn't that far from New York, where Sally had relatives and was situated on Lake Ontario.

Toronto is also the most cosmopolitan city in the world. It was very interesting with large Jewish, Italian, Chinese and Vietnamese sections of the city, in addition to a large British ex patriot culture. In the accounts and administration department was a Jewish lad and ladies from the Philippines, Sri Lanka, Germany, Denmark and Hong Kong. Those from overseas seemed to outnumber the Brits and Canadians.

Sally was in tears as I left, but it was only for eight months and I needed to get the yearning for travel (and excitement) out of my system. I can still remember getting on the plane at Heathrow. I was also fighting back the tears, but at the same time looking forward to an exciting project and a new beginning.

As soon as I settled in Mississauga (the native Inuit Indian word for "rattle snake"), I joined a squash club. This gave me a social life, where I could escape from work at weekends and where I soon made a few friends. Sport provides an excellent opportunity to socialise and make friends, especially when moving to an overseas land or new area.

I was popular with most of the staff and soon made lifelong friends at work. I'm still in constant touch with Geoff, the Toronto branch Sales Manager and Betty Ann, the division's IT Manager. Geoff and his wife Anne invited me to stay at their house a few times. They came from Scarborough, Yorkshire and we shared the same British sense of humour.

At the time Geoff had two lovely young daughters Naomi and Katy. In 2008, nearly twenty years on, I was invited to Naomi's wedding in Chicago. Geoff sent Naomi a draft of his father of the bride speech, which I had written and included as many, relevant, but inappropriate jokes as possible. Naomi guessed straight away who had written it and immediately banned Geoff and me from getting anywhere near a microphone. We had many great laughs.

Cab visited for a two week holiday in the summer and this provided good company. In the autumn my friends Richard (my former marathon partner) and Helen visited and got married in Niagara. Sally also visited for two weeks soon after Cab and we had a good time, travelling by car to visit her mother and two sisters in New York. It was my first visit to New York, so we did all the usual sightseeing visits.

Although I· had a lot of work pressure by then, it did strengthen our relationship. I remember phoning Sally soon after she returned to England and asking her how she was. She just replied "…. (pause) very lonely". She was lovely, caring, honest and just what I needed at that time.

Everyone loved Sally when she visited the workplaces in Toronto and Mississauga. One lady commented how lovely she was and then asked me "what did your parents think when they knew you were going out with a black girl". I jokingly replied "they didn't mind the fact that she was black, but they were furious when they found out she was an accountant". I used that line quite a lot.

There was plenty of mirth during my stay in Toronto and the office staff enjoyed my role as "the eccentric Englishman". Each Monday they would ask me "how did the Baggies (West Bromwich Albion FC) get on?". If the Baggies had won I used to buy everyone doughnuts. We had a poor season, "still languishing in mediocrity" as one of my old teachers used to say, so it didn't cost me too much.

One Monday I came in to the office, after the Baggies beat West Ham away, and replied "we stuffed the Cockney B*st*rds". All the British men understood and laughed. The ladies just smiled at my eccentricity and one asked "what are the Cockney B*st*rds?". I said oh "it's just the nickname of an English football team, like you have the Toronto Blue Jays and New York Yankees".

I then added "actually the UK Divisional FD is one". I was horrified when the UK Divisional FD, from the Kingston head office did visit. The lady from Sri Lanka walked up to him with a smile and said "Paul tells me you like the Cockney B*st*rds". I then had to explain that one away.

The President of the Canadian operation could be very moody and at times aggressive, especially after arguments with his wife, who worked as his secretary. However, I felt as though I was "bullet proof". He knew I was good at my job, was making significant improvements and that he wouldn't be able to get anyone better in the short term. Anyway, I would be returning home in a matter of a few months. So I admit, I had a bit of what I thought of as harmless, but slightly mischievous, fun at his expense.

One day the President came in to the office wearing a pink tie with small brown spots in lines. He was balding and had just had a hair transplant operation. The top of his balding head had been caught by the sun and was pink and there were small reddish brown scabs in perfect rows, where new hair had been implanted. I just couldn't resist saying "oh Mike, you've got a matching head and tie set".

The office staff just erupted with laughter and Mike fled into his office with a face like thunder. He remained there all day. His wife later admitted he had been too embarrassed to come out of his office after my gag. Fortunately, I got away with it and it became another of those fond memories of my Canadian adventure.

I did return for a (jet lagged) holiday to Britain at Christmas. It was good to see Sally, my family and friends again. It was also the second birthday of my lovely niece Danielle. I bought her a cuddly, beautifully coloured toy parrot from Toronto. Danielle called it "Polly Carrot from Cadana", she was just beginning to speak and string a few words together.

However, my "working holiday" wasn't all fun and excitement. The VP Finance was a workaholic, often working from early in the morning through into the early hours of the next day. There were virtually no files or working papers to follow, the level of (financial) control was (in my professional opinion) poor and there was a lack of good management information. Also, how to improve many of the group objectives, such as how to reduce working capital and increase the return on capital employed (ROCE), hadn't been communicated to management.

The control of cash was also (in my opinion) poor and within a few weeks of my arriving there was a significant bad debt. I think it was £100k +. This attracted the attention of the divisional directors. The workload I inherited was also significant. For example the VP Finance was in the habit of personally organising and overseeing the computer backup in Mississauga every night, just before midnight.

The significant inherited workload, lack of anyone to delegate to, and need for improvements, meant I ended up working long hours. The only person who I could delegate to was Betty Ann. I left her completely in charge of all computer related matters, while just performing a management and monitoring role of IT myself. Betty Ann became a great friend and ally. I worked late with her on the computer month-end routines. In reality Betty Ann did all the work and I bought pizza and kept her company.

I also needed to fight a few "battles" with the MD to make the point that working all hours and carrying out computer back-ups until late at night had just contributed to an overall lack of control and would prevent me from resolving the real priorities. I think I managed to win most of the "discussions", although I often needed to be very persistent.

Fortunately, I did make significant improvements in the overall level of financial control and the quality of management information, as well as reducing borrowings and bad debts, thus improving the ROCE. I'm sure that, professionally, my working stint in Canada was regarded as a great success. However, on a personal level it was at times very tough.

Voluntary Services Overseas (VSO) advises its candidates to expect some difficult times. It is usual for volunteers to really enjoy the first few weeks abroad as they will probably be in an exciting and exotic place. However, they then often take a dip, as they experience life far away from family, friends and loved ones. Loneliness will often then set in, as they also have to cope with massive changes in their jobs, homes and friendships (or lack of them).

After a few months volunteers adjust to their new surroundings, job and friends, making it difficult to then adjust to returning home. I experienced my "dip" at the same time as I started working long hours and felt under great pressure to improve the level of financial control.

This short stint abroad taught me quite a few valuable lessons. Usually we live our lives fluctuating between excitement and despondency depending upon whether or not we consider our external conditions and experiences to be good or bad. However, the world will never be completely to our liking and consequently we experience highs and lows.

The Dalai Lama, when asked what surprised him most about humanity, answered "Man. Because he sacrifices his health in order to make money. Then he sacrifices money to recuperate his health. And then he is so anxious about the future that he does not enjoy the present; the result being that he does not live in the present or the future; he lives as if he is never going to die, and then dies having never really lived". I was learning this from my own experience.

I had big ups and downs in Canada and although I'm grateful for the experience, it cured me of any wish to travel. I was beginning to learn that **"happiness is within"**. The philosopher Schumacher says that it is **difficult to find happiness within yourself, but it's impossible to find it anywhere else**. Soon, I would learn that it is impossible to be happy, regardless of the external circumstances, unless you have inner peace.

The crucial question is then, what conditions need to be in place in order to have inner peace? I was still searching and by a process of elimination, I was learning what didn't lead to happiness. Paradoxically, whatever I had been conditioned to believe would be a cause of happiness, my experiences proved wouldn't in themselves result in it e.g. money, qualifications, career, travel, drinking and partying, having a beautiful partner etc.

Despite my continual search, I was unable to find the pot of gold at the end of the rainbow that happiness represented. Fortunately, I would soon get all the answers I needed to improve my life.

A Link with Olivia

In approximately 1990, I had a rare visit to the doctor. I was sitting in the waiting room and noticed Olivia's mother at the other end of the room, also seated and waiting for an appointment. I got up and walked towards her to say hello. I was popular with Olivia's parents and expected a warm response, although I was a bit nervous. They had commented on occasions that they hoped we would end up together long term and get married.

As I got close, my name was announced over the public address system. She hadn't recognised me, but when my name was mentioned she hurriedly stared at the floor. This was approximately fourteen years after we had split up and she was a bit agitated and clearly wanted to avoid me.

I was a bit disappointed, but I didn't take it personally. The one thing that was apparent was the extent of the upset and the effect it had had on the whole family, as well as me. To me this was one of the clearest indicators of just how deeply Olivia had been keen on me. I'm sure my deep love had been reciprocated. Regrettably, I had completely lost touch with Olivia. Anyway, I still didn't know for sure if her strong feelings for me had turned sour or not.

Ben and Nick

It was around this time that Ben phoned me to tell me that Nick was getting married. I think Ben was the best man and he was organising the stag night. Ben invited me to attend. I politely declined, but Ben kept asking and became quite persistent. In the end Ben got quite short and angry with me.

Nick was getting married to Lyn, a slim, petite and attractive lady. Lyn worked with Nick's brother Chris and Nick first met her when we both attended a party together. Lyn passed a message via Chris and Nick that she fancied me. I think this must have been in late 1978 and we had a few dates. However, this was unfair on Lyn as I still only wanted Olivia. Now Nick and Lyn must have been dating for a while. I think they are still married and I wish them well.

There was little point in me attending the stag night. I wasn't being nasty. There was simply no basis for a friendship with

Nick. The trust and respect had gone. Also, most importantly, I had to get on with my life and I didn't want continual reminders of my most difficult and painful period.

I was surprised that Nick continually thought that he could just walk back into my life and expected me to treat him as though we were great friends still. Ben also continually tried to involve me and Nick in some social events together. Clearly he also just expected me to act as though Nick was still a close friend.

I can remember some years earlier the first time I saw Nick after he had gone out for his few dates with Olivia. Ben brought him to one of the parties at my first house. I opened the door to see Nick with a broad grin. I muttered something like "you weren't invited (pause)". I then relented and said "oh well you may as well come in".

In the late 1980s and/or early 1990s Ben had organised some games of doubles tennis, with us playing together against Nick and another friend. I did try to get the friendship back on track, but I really did find it tough. I simply didn't want this permanent reminder of past hurt. I really did need a fresh life.

What did they think my opinion of Nick would be? Like Olivia, did they genuinely believe I didn't care about her and wouldn't be hurt? But if they genuinely believed I wouldn't be hurt, why did they disappear from my life for such a long period?

Even now, I would find it extremely difficult to like Nick as I used to do. However, this would be the most beneficial mind and outcome for everyone. I might be able to forgive Nick and to not have any resentment towards him, but trusting and accepting him would still be very difficult.

I still need to avoid those reminders of my past trauma. Similarly, Nick could easily have helped Olivia and I become reconciled, as we both wanted. His meddling in our lives caused a big complication and had a devastating effect. As a result of these actions, I am sure Olivia suffered greatly, as I had done. The impact of Nick's action had been truly massive in providing a barrier to prevent us getting back together again.

I know I shouldn't be surprised by anyone acting out of self interest. However, I still find Nick's actions to be totally inexcusable. His disloyal, deceitful and covetous behaviour was totally contrary to my own view of how friends should support and help one another. My problem with Olivia had probably given him his ideal and only brief opportunity.

I expect that Nick had tried it on with Olivia previously behind my back, but without any joy. Although the betrayal and loss of friendship, with him and others, was hurtful, the most damaging effect was that it gave me the belief that Olivia may now be trying to hurt me and that I may have lost my chance with her. It was as though she might be figuratively sticking two fingers up at me. I had simply been too badly hurt to risk any possibility of further pain and I had few friends to turn to.

In this respect **the real enemy was my mind of hurt, uncontrolled desires, fear and pride**. Bodhisattva Shantideva says "there is nothing to fear other than my mind". He goes on to say:

> *"In this (world) unsubdued and crazed elephants*
> *Are incapable of causing such harms*
> *As the miseries of the deepest hell*
> *Which can be caused by the unleashed elephant*
> *of mind."*

I will write more on this subject after my fortieth birthday party in 1994.

My Father's Death

In 1992 my father died at the age of sixty-four. He had been in poor health since his first heart attack in 1977, some fifteen years earlier. He had been a heavy smoker. He didn't drink much, but he had little physical exercise and his main hobby was building businesses, which just caused him great stress. In his later years his time was spent working voluntarily for a local Farm Animal Sanctuary.

Three months before he died he had a stroke, resulting in a loss of speech and less physical mobility. Officially he died of a heart attack. In recent years, while rescuing the family business, we had been through a lot together, so his death was a great loss. He was a very well respected man and the funeral service was packed with people wishing to show their respects.

I got a call from my mother when he died. I was working in London at the time and had to return to my hotel, book out and collect all my belongings, before driving back to the family home in the Midlands. I had been in a bit of a state when I packed my clothes and checked out at the hotel.

When I unpacked at home, I realised I had left a shirt and tie back at the hotel. I can also remember being in a state of denial as I drove up the M1, constantly going over what my mother had said, to establish whether I had interpreted things correctly or not. This is another example of how everything that appears to mind is "mere appearance" or "illusion".

When I arrived home mother and Sally were there to greet me. Sally threw her arms around me and gave me a hug. She had left work as soon as she had been told the news. She is a very caring person, so I wouldn't have expected anything else. Unfairly, her boss complained about her taking time off as "we weren't even married". That seemed very harsh on a hard working and very competent employee. The MD was racist and I think the FD was looking for excuses to give her a hard time.

After the funeral the family decided to scatter the ashes in the nearby woods where my father used to walk most days with Fatima. We decided to scatter them from a bridge into the stream below. All our thoughts were on my father and nobody had noticed that Fatima had gone missing.

I was reminiscing about my father as we stood on the bridge, about to scatter the ashes. As we dropped Dad's remains into the flowing water below, Fatima suddenly appeared from under the bridge. She was walking down stream and was covered by the ashes. It was a poignant moment as though loving master and dog couldn't and wouldn't be parted even by the finality of death. I thought it was a fitting end and one that my father would have been happy with.

At this stage in my life I wasn't good at dealing with my emotions and I don't think I dealt with bereavement very well. As usual my independent, decisive nature dealt with all the practicalities like the probate. However, I probably just suppressed the emotions, a strategy that would just store problems for the future.

My mother dealt with things as well as anyone can. I am sure the many years of meditation must have helped. This contrasts sharply with a friend of mine, whose mother-in-law hit the bottle after her husband died and is now a chronic alcoholic, still blaming the death of her partner for her unhappiness.

One lady I know, soon after her husband died said "I've now had three days of grieving, I've had a good marriage, I'll never get married again, but now I've got to get on with the rest of my life". Many people faced with the same problem had reacted in very different ways.

Apart from meditation, in difficult circumstances such as bereavement, it would be very useful to have the benefit of having studied the wisdom of great teachers. Understanding the difference between love and attachment would help a great deal. Pure love never causes any pain whatsoever. However, desirous attachment, which is self centred, will always result in suffering. Bereavement must be very difficult to deal with. Unfortunately, the attachment will result in what I describe as "grieving for oneself".

The sufferings of birth, sickness, ageing and death are inevitable and include the loss of loved ones. **The pain is inevitable, but the extent of suffering is optional**.

It wouldn't be long before I was introduced to meditation and the wisdom needed to deal with problems and reduce suffering. I would soon learn that pain is inevitable with an uncontrolled mind and uncontrolled life. Controlling the mind would provide the answers that I had been searching for and would make the past suffering regrettable, but necessary and worthwhile.

Sally

In 1992 I took another big step in changing my life, when I became vegetarian. Sally and I were on holiday on one of the Greek islands and I read a book by Jonathon Porritt, former director of Friends of the Earth. Porritt talked about the major problems in the world and shared his views and discussed solutions. In one chapter he discussed the problems of over-population and of the world's population growing to unsustainable levels. He said that double the world's population could be fed if everyone was vegetarian.

I had been considering going vegetarian for some time. My brother Cab had already been vegan for a few years, and my mother had been vegetarian for even longer. My father had recently gone vegetarian, although this was a bit of a problem because, by his own admission, he didn't like vegetables. It was typical of my father who could be quite eccentric.

I mentioned to Sally that I was thinking of going vegetarian and she said that she was as well. This made the decision simple; we could both go vegetarian at the same time and would be able to support one another. Sally was a great cook, so there were plenty of new dishes to look forward to.

People often ask me why I went vegetarian and I say "all the reasons". I was concerned about the conditions that captive animals were kept in to provide food. There was also much talk about artificially pumping animals with hormones to "fatten" them up, ready for human consumption. Health reasons also encouraged me to give up meat, and there was still a scare about BSE ("mad cow disease") and the latent ("ticking time bomb") threat to humans of variant CJD.

Regarding BSE, it seems absolutely inconceivable to me that we could feed vegetarian cows with dead sheep's infected carcases and be surprised when problems arise. This was all done to reduce cost and improve profit, regardless of the problems these actions would create. Man does increasingly cause problems by assuming he can improve upon and control nature, purely for monetary benefit. The motivation for these actions is also based on the false premise that money is a cause of happiness.

My motto is "**nature knows best**" and I agree with the philosophy of trying to live in harmony with nature, rather than trying to control it. Why do we make life difficult and create problems by constantly trying to "paddle up stream" and then be surprised by the results?

I am not naïve enough to think that by not eating meat I will save people from starvation. However, contributing to a problem made me feel uncomfortable. Sometimes people would say things like "you giving up meat won't save the starving masses will it?". I regard that argument as being a bit like saying there's no point in not committing murder or theft, because it'll have virtually no impact on the world's crime rate. We still have to do what we feel comfortable with, what fits in with our guidelines on moral discipline and what will help others, including animals.

Currently, much land that could be used to grow cereal and food for the population is used to grow food for animals, which in turn feed people in wealthy countries. If everyone stopped eating meat, this wouldn't in itself save the world's population from starvation.

There would be other issues that would also need to be resolved to feed people in poor and developing nations, such as a redistribution of wealth and resources, better education, better provision of technology and training, a reduction in the indebtedness of the poor nations, reducing the buying power of food supermarket companies in the wealthy nations etc. My view is that there is no point in exacerbating a problem, or indulging in a course of action that I feel is wrong and that may directly or indirectly lead to suffering.

One year later, Sally and I split up, or at least that was when the decision was made. We continued to live together until early 1994, when I started my new job as an executive at the head office of the plc I worked for. This was a group role rather than a divisional role, and was based at the head office in Birmingham. It had the added advantage of being largely office based and meant far less travel.

Sally and I had had a difficult time. In particular, Sally was still trying to qualify as an accountant and worked very long hours in the evenings and at weekends, in addition to her full time job. She had also had to deal with failing exams and losing jobs on a number of occasions. The pressure had been difficult for her and the strain did tell.

Since returning from Canada, I had been travelling all over the country, frequently staying away from home. Even when I did stay at home, I frequently set off very early to work in another city and wouldn't return until late, when Sally was often still studying and/or revising for her exams. Although we were living in my single bedroom apartment, we simply didn't see enough of one another or have sufficient quality time together.

It had been a difficult time for me with working long hours and a lot of work-related travel. In recent years, I had been working in a job I didn't much like. Unfortunately, the recession was quite deep and I hadn't been able to find alternative work. Much of my time had been spent in airports, staying in hotels and travelling on motorways. It was tiring and lonely.

The split came shortly after a holiday in Corfu. Sally had felt the stress of sitting her final exams and had also recently lost her job, in difficult circumstances. At least losing her job had enabled her to devote even more study time to her final exams and this time she passed them. She became a qualified accountant and I was very pleased for her. I knew how much effort she had put into qualifying, which is a major achievement and how much it meant to her.

For my part, I can blame the lack of contentment in my mind as the major contributory factor in the split. It was too easy to split up after the stress Sally had been under and the fact that I wasn't enjoying my job and the long hours it entailed. I must admit, I also still had some protective barriers around myself after the split and problems with Olivia. Although these protective layers were supposed to help me avoid further hurt, they would also prevent me getting too close to any other partner.

Everyone thought Sally was a lovely person and I still have the greatest respect and affection for her. We lived together until early 1994 and stayed in touch for a few months while

Sally sought reconciliation. Fortunately, she soon met and married a solid and reliable new partner. I'm sure he has been able to give her all the things I couldn't.

I believe people come into your life at certain times, as and when it is necessary to do so and to help provide life's lessons. Sally helped me a lot as I came out of my most difficult period. She is a lovely person and gave me love and comradeship. She was always completely loyal and honest. I hope she is very happy now and I'll always appreciate my time with her.

This probably remains the only time, since I was about twenty-four, that I have ended a serious relationship. Usually, the relationships just fizzled out, with both of us drifting apart and there being no real pain for either party. However, I was upset about how much ending the relationship had hurt Sally.

I wrestled with this issue and the unease it caused for some time. I had been badly hurt myself in the past and later I resolved not to cause anymore unnecessary hurt to any lady. I now don't date very often and if I do, it has to be on the basis that I see the lady as a potential long term partner.

5

Life Begins at Forty
(1994)

Back in the dark days of 1979 I set out to make myself "tough", to avoid any future hurt. In 1994 I would soon learn that **what makes a man strong is starting with a pure intention and then making sure that thoughts, words and deeds are in harmony**. Previously, after the problems with Olivia, I'd been thinking one thing, saying nothing (retreating into my cave when hurt) and acting differently, as though I was perfectly all right (giving the impression I didn't care).

Ego just always gets in the way. No wonder I made a mess of things. If we live a pure, truthful life in harmony with the external environment (without looking for a result), everything works out fine. Why do we keep trying to paddle upstream? What a pity we don't have (access to) wisdom when we are young. Youth really is wasted on the young!

For me life really did begin at forty and there was much change. Firstly, in 1994 I split up with Sally. On the one hand, I missed her companionship and support, but equally I looked forward to a new start in life. Work-wise, after five and a half years, I moved from one of the divisions of the plc I was employed by to the group head office. Life was certainly changing significantly.

Following the Cadbury code on corporate governance, the group I was working for was expanding its internal audit capability and trying to improve its internal (financial) controls. I was appointed as Group Internal Auditor. This represented a significant promotion and I was on a head office executive contract, with six months notice. Consequently, I also had significant job security, or so I thought.

As Group Internal Auditor, I was working alongside Derek, the Group Internal Computer Auditor. It was a good partnership. Derek was a Chartered Accountant but his background and specialism was Computer Audit. I was strong on Financial Controls and we worked well together. Derek was also in overall charge of all Group Internal Audit matters.

I knew there was more to life than money, stress and pressure, but I didn't know what. I was becoming aware that happiness goes beyond material well being. Fortunately, I wouldn't have to wait too long before I would discover the answers.

I had always intended to retire at fifty and this new job would help me towards that goal providing security for some of those years. I would then be able to plan the rest of my life with the financial independence and security to do whatever I wanted to do. That was my thinking anyway.

Corporate Progression

One of the early projects in my new group role was to help a Divisional Internal Auditor conduct an internal audit at one of her division's subsidiaries. The subsidiary Finance Director was a lady Meryl with a reputation for being very aggressive.

The first day involved a very routine work programme that included a review of the cash sales system at one of the branches. When we started the second morning the subsidiary

FD phoned me and was very aggressive and critical. She had also been highly critical of me to the Divisional FD and to my boss Derek.

I was concerned and had mixed feelings about this. On the one hand it wasn't pleasant to be criticised to senior management, who invariably would influence my career. On the other hand her behaviour was so "over the top" that I wondered if it was an indicator of fraud or major weaknesses being covered up.

Many weeks later Meryl was still criticising me to any senior person who would listen. I was beginning to get very tired and annoyed with this behaviour. Derek then commented "methinks the lady doth protest too much". We later became aware of instances of weak cash sales systems being exploited fraudulently by staff and of significant book debt assets that couldn't be reconciled properly, which would inevitably lead to significant loss.

I received quite a bit of training about fraud and then had significant experience of detecting and investigating it. Frauds are rarely detected by internal or external auditors. The most common method of finding out about fraud is after a whistle-blower has talked. For example a buyer, committing fraud, might be having an affair with a female secretary and after she is jilted, she then informs other managers.

The possibility and likelihood of people committing fraud roughly follows a normal distribution curve. Roughly speaking twenty-five per cent of people are totally honest, and the same percentage are totally dishonest and are always looking to exploit an opportunity. The other fifty per cent or so are basically honest people, but in certain circumstances and if opportunity exists they could turn to crime.

It is a frightening statistic that companies need to guard against three quarters of their staff and they don't know which three quarters. This is why it is essential for companies to operate a tight control culture with effective financial systems and controls. Examples are division of duties, management monitoring, authorisation procedures, budgetary control etc. Weak systems and controls will increase the possibility of fraud occurring.

The sort of circumstances that increase the likelihood of people committing fraud are drink, drugs and gambling problems, money problems, divorce etc. Derek often mentioned "lifestyle audits". By this he would mean have a "healthy cynicism" if a member of staff suddenly starts spending a significant amount on fancy cars, has expensive holidays or lives a celebrity type lifestyle etc.

I found the greatest indicators of fraud were extreme and/or aggressive behaviour, staff being overly defensive, frequent non adherence to systems and controls and/or arguing that such systems are unnecessary and/or won't work.

I have missed frauds, warned management about the possibility of frauds, assisted fraud investigations and helped detect them. Thankfully, I have always learnt from them. Often good, relevant experience is gained from the mistakes. I have also found that staff and management don't want to believe fraud could be occurring and I was probably like that myself when I was less experienced. Similarly staff and management will often overlook extreme behaviour and actually make excuses for staff like "oh, it's just the way Jim is!".

Our main role was to ensure the group's financial controls were adequate and effective, thus reducing the risk of loss. This came under the broad heading of corporate governance. However, I would always advise management not to overlook such "fraud indicators". Fraud was not the only thing we were involved in, but it was the most interesting part of our work.

40th Birthday Party

In the June it was my fortieth birthday. I fancied having a big party to celebrate this landmark occasion, which also represented my life moving in different directions. I wanted to invite a diversity of friends from different periods in my life.

I soon worked out that my mother and Sally were also kindly planning a surprise party. I told them I welcomed this and suggested I review the guest list to ensure all those I considered to be special would be invited. I didn't intend to invite Nick, but my mother and Sally talked me into doing so. They didn't know the full story.

I wasn't being nasty, the dynamics had simply changed and there was no way that we would be able to go back to being close friends, regardless of what he (Nick) may have wanted or expected. Also, I simply didn't want permanent reminders around me of my darkest period and the greatest trauma (by far) in my life. I needed to move on.

The party was a success. There were friends there from the squash club, junior school, grammar school, boy scouts, various football teams, polytechnic, my previous divisional job and now my new group role. There were also many relatives. We filled the lounge at the tennis and squash club with the capacity of about ninety people.

For me the night was just soured by one incident. This was another hurtful reminder of the greatest trauma in my life. Nick and Ben left their table to talk to Bill. I heard Bill say to Nick "how are you mate, I haven't seen you since (pause), well since you went out with Olivia?". My ears pricked up and I turned to see Nick grinning from ear to ear, gloating about his (minor) apparent success.

I noticed Ben was also grinning while shaking his head in apparent admiration, as if to say "well done mate, I don't know how you do it, you certainly managed to pull a cracking looking girl there". There seemed to be no recognition of or concern whatsoever for the damage caused to me (or Olivia).

I felt all the hurt again. I felt this situation was disrespectful to Olivia, as it reduced her merely to an object of lust and desire. I felt it was also insensitive and disrespectful to me at my party. It seemed as though Olivia had been treated as a prize trophy with no concern about her wishes and feelings, or my own. The usual etiquette of friendship simply didn't apply. The disruption to two people's lives and the resultant misery caused seemed to be of no importance.

It was another reminder about the scene with Caesar, Brutus and a conspirator. I sarcastically thought, "Yes! Well done Nick, you managed to get a few dates with a very pretty girl, who happened to be the former partner of one of your best friends". "You were thrown a few scraps by someone who was probably at a very low point, and was very upset with a close friend of yours, who she wanted to be reunited with, while she mistakenly thought he didn't care". "You did nothing to help us and you gained little apart from pride".

What Nick did gain was far outweighed by the hurt and suffering caused to others and the obstacles to Olivia and myself achieving our goals and wishes to be together. His actions, which resulted from a covetous mind, had had a major effect on the lives of two people. They had probably changed those two lives significantly.

I had always compared Nick's values with my own. I had never gone out with the partner of a friend and still haven't to this day. When Olivia split up with Neil, I had met up with him to explain that I wanted to go out with her and endeavoured to minimise any hurt. Nick, on the other hand, had got involved with Olivia in a very underhand manner that would only cause hurt and suffering and from which there would be no winners. He had immediately dropped me, at my lowest point and traded our years of friendship for a few crumbs.

Over the years, I had compared Nick's actions to finding a very close friend in a bad way physically and deciding to take advantage, giving him a good kicking and taking his wallet. On finding the wallet only contained a fiver he decided to spend it anyway and years later expected his friend to welcome him back.

I thought to myself, I wonder if Nick ever had a similar problem with his wife, who incorrectly thought he didn't care about her, what would he (Nick) think if a friend of his, hearing the news, immediately hit on her. Similarly, would Ben have been so impressed with and proud of Nick, if he (Nick) had been hitting on his (Ben's) wife as soon as it became public that they had a problem to overcome?

Nick's reaction did not surprise me. However, the greatest disappointment was from Ben's attitude. Later, at a friend's funeral in 2012 Ben gave one of the speeches. He said that Gaz, Ben and I were always together throughout Grammar school. "Always the three of us were together, always just the three of us". It was true.

After leaving school Ben and I were in constant touch. When I had my problems with Olivia in 1979 and I was at rock bottom Ben disappeared. I didn't hear from him again until he wrote to me at Polytechnic approximately ten months later. I gave him the benefit of the doubt and assumed he had declared neutrality. Maybe he had just wanted to keep his head below the parapet rather than risk getting caught in the cross fire.

Unfortunately, this response looked like evidence that Ben had given active encouragement to Nick to chase after Olivia. This was a great disappointment. I thought about Ben "why did you accept and seemingly support Nick's behaviour, when you would have been outraged if it had happened to you?".

I can only state my views on the matter, which come from a very hurt mind. No doubt every reader will have his or her own opinion on the morals involved and the rights and wrongs. I list some of the issues below and leave readers to arrive at their own conclusion:

Could and should close friends try to help two former partners who still want to be together? Is it acceptable to abandon a close friend, who will probably be at a very low point, while making a move, or supporting another friend hitting on, your friend's former partner? Should you maintain loyalty to a very close friend, who has done you no harm, while he and his partner are going through difficulties?

Does the fact that a former partner of a friend is exceptionally good looking make any difference to your loyalty and responsibility to him or her? Is it ok to just consider a very good looking lady as a "prize trophy", ignoring the feelings and wishes of her and her former partner?

How important are openness, honesty, trust and respect in any friendship/relationship? Are they prerequisites of all true friendships and pillars to support any good relationship? Had I overstated their importance? Should I be able to continue friendships as I had before?

How do we weigh up loyalty and helping others, compared to looking after ourselves? Is all fair in love and war? Is only looking after ourselves going to lead to happiness? What kind of world will we live in if it is "dog eat dog" and won't everyone suffer?

Can we trust our own moral compass? Will our actions be justified by our desires and the ethics be tailored accordingly? Where can we get our moral guidance from? Can we sum up such issues by always treating others as we would wish to be treated?

Did I deserve to be treated in such a way, because of my nervousness, lack of confidence and inability to open up? Did I deserve to be abandoned and criticised and (sometimes deliberately) hurt, because I had dealt with the matter so poorly? Had I missed my opportunity with Olivia, making it acceptable for anyone, regardless of past loyalties, friendships and our wishes to be together, to make a move for her?

Certainly the chain of events that unravelled had led to no winners. I had definitely got things badly wrong, but hadn't most others also done the same?

From my point of view should I welcome back friends, who I feel have abandoned me or wronged me, causing great hurt, regardless of the circumstances? Should I be "big" enough to forgive and forget and to not judge or criticise? If not the person, is it ok to criticise their actions?

Nowadays, if ever I find myself in a moral dilemma, such as had occurred with my friends in the past, I always try the approach of being "open and honest with everyone". If I can marry this with not looking for a result for myself, I invariably find that everything works out fine. I will enlarge upon this later in the book.

This was my fortieth birthday party and I now had another reminder of all those years of upset, coupled with (my perceived) betrayal and/or abandonment by friends. When was it all going to end? Fifteen years after the event and I was still being handicapped by this ball and chain that was a constant reminder of my past hurt and suffering.

It was then that I made the decision to escape from these manacles, cut myself free and no longer mix with anyone from the past who had failed to support me during the lowest point in my life. After this night there would be no scenes, just a "moving on".

I wish everyone from my youth and early to mid twenties well. Equally, it is important for myself and others, that I don't hold on to any resentment. However, if anyone from this era wants to know how much I valued their friendship, they can carry out a simple self assessment and mark themselves out of ten, with the following two questions:

Firstly, how much help and support was given to me when I was at my lowest point in 1979? Secondly, during our upset, how much badly needed assistance was given to Olivia and myself, to enable us to overcome our difficulties and effect a reconciliation? There weren't many who would score more than nil for either matter.

Back in 1979 I had been naive in expecting friends to rally round. Friends are transient and will be motivated by self interest. As life evolves and unravels we naturally make new acquaintances. This is merely part of the impermanence of all phenomena. There would be new friends without all the baggage from the past. There would be no more tennis with Ben and Nick. Instead I would concentrate on playing at my Club, joining the leagues and making new tennis buddies.

At the end of the party I did something I wasn't proud of. I don't think I had ever criticised Nick to anyone and have always tried to act with dignity. However, it has been difficult for me to do so.

As Nick was about to leave he came across to shake my hand. I took his hand but gave him a dirty look. It was hardly as dramatic as the fight scene between Colin Firth and Hugh Grant in "Bridget Jones's Diary". However, he would have been under no doubt that I wasn't impressed with him or his actions. His wife just said "come on let's go". I now rarely see Nick and don't think I've spoken to him since.

I continued to meet Ben at the football matches with Tim, Cab and Ben's son Tom. However, a few years later Ben stopped attending. He had decided to protest about the price increases. It was typical of Ben, who was very price conscious and like me, could be quite stubborn. The only loser was probably Ben. These days I just see Ben occasionally, as we get older it'll probably just be a case of "four funerals and a wedding".

I'll summarise the relationship with Ben as having merely led to a "disappointment" and leave it at that. Friendships were never going to be the same again. At the end of the day, I wish everyone well and still do. I simply didn't want these constant reminders of the lowest point in my life. I simply needed to protect myself from any more upset.

It would be easy to blame Nick for all the pain I had endured. However, all this hurt was in my mind and had been created by it. In reality, no enemy can be as vicious and destructive as our own minds, when negative states such as anger, hatred, pride, depression, desirous attachment, resentment and jealousy prevail.

The reality was that I had allowed Nick to cause me pain and increase the fear of more suffering. I had allowed Nick's betrayal to hurt me. In turn I had allowed the ensuing abandonment by other friends and hostility from some people to upset me more. Similarly, I had allowed these incidents to get inside my head and create a perception that Olivia may be trying to hurt me. I reasoned it may well have been a case that "hell hath no fury like a woman (who thinks she has been) scorned".

Nick's actions were always going to create a complication, but I had built them up in my mind to such a degree that I had feared approaching Olivia, to ensure I couldn't get hurt any more. Regrettably, this instinctive survival strategy had merely prevented me from winning back what was most important (i.e. Olivia).

The mind is a very good servant, but a very poor master. In reality I actually needed to learn how to control my mind.

Your mind is the creator of your world and your reality. It was my mind that was the real villain and what had created my hurt and suffering. It had felt as though Olivia and Nick had stuck two fingers up at me, but the real battleground had been in my mind. There were many lessons to learn, but now I was getting closer to the answers.

My Kind Teacher and Holy Spiritual Guide

Throughout this book I have avoided getting personal about anyone including Nick, whose actions I believed had contributed to significant loss and had led to great hurt. However, I have said what my thoughts and feelings were at the time. Wherever these views are incorrect I have tried to balance matters with the "correct view".

The correct view comes from (Buddha's) wisdom and is always the most beneficial view, both for myself and others. This is the virtuous view that will always result in a calm, peaceful, relaxed mind. I would soon be learning all the techniques and practices to achieve such a controlled mind. However, to balance my comments in the previous chapter, this seems to be the best place to discuss how I need to practise in order to let go of all the pain relating to the past.

It could be said that Nick has been my teacher and has provided me with many opportunities to learn and develop. As such, and in order to provide a balanced view, I am now listing the lessons which are relevant. Although out of chronological sequence, regarding when I learnt the wisdom, I think this is the most appropriate place to comment on these lessons and practices for my mind.

Forgiveness doesn't mean changing the view that wrongs have been done. It means letting go of the emotional charge of feeling wronged. I would have been the greatest beneficiary of letting go of all resentment.

I still believe Nick's actions were totally inexcusable. However, I also know that he should have provided me with little more than an irritation or nuisance. His actions affected my mind and this is what led to the suffering. I should still have been able to overcome the pain and to talk to Olivia and get the desired outcome. At the end of the day, I alone am responsible for the state of my mind and for all the outcomes in my life.

Back in 1979 and the 1980s my mind had been very negative, as well as being full of hurt and the fear of more suffering. Anxiety, dread, apprehension, worry, fear and panic are all mental states. To observe and recognise fear when it arises enables us to see it change and move on. The awareness that contains fear is not fearful itself. There is a need to be separate from the fear, not identify with it and to watch it drift away, like a cloud in the sky.

The sky will always remain a perfect blue expanse. There is room in the sky for the occasional storm and just as a storm or black cloud does not have the power to destroy the sky, so a negative thought or feeling doesn't have the ability to destroy the mind.

Bodhisattva Shantideva says about worries and problems:

> *"If the problem can be solved, why worry?*
> *If the problem can-not be solved, worrying will do*
> *you no good"*

The world will not be as anyone wants it, so it is important to learn to practise acceptance. The above lines of reasoning will also help, if there is a belief that worrying will not help the situation and will only cause unhappiness.

The first stage in controlling the mind is to observe the mind and I needed to learn how to do this and to practise it

177

continually. In particular, resentment against Nick would only harm me and needed to be eliminated. Having resentment could be said to be like picking a coal from a fire to throw at an enemy. Invariably it will cause you, the person with the resentment, the most harm and not the (perceived) enemy.

These changes in friendships were really the beginning of understanding the **impermanence** of all phenomena. With a negative, impure and uncontrolled mind, friends do become enemies and enemies become friends. Also, everything that is a cause of happiness can also be a cause of suffering (to an uncontrolled mind). Consequently, there is the need to understand and practise **acceptance**. This is simply the way it is.

When facing difficulties I had expected help, support and loyalty from my friends. However, at my lowest point, I felt I had been merely the victim of hindrance, abandonment, deceit and covetous behaviour. Were my expectations unreasonable?

People will act out of self interest. This is also simply the way it is. Friends' egos will always necessitate that they will value their perceived needs above those of others. Similarly, friends will only be friends in so far as they can gain from friendships. Why should it be any other way?

I also needed to understand that I was not the centre of the Universe and what right had I got to expect friends to put my needs first? All these years **I had taken myself too seriously**. My own ego had created division. There are seven billion people on this planet. Paul Webb's needs and desires would never be the sole priority and externalities would never satisfy these desires all the time.

There is a line of reason which helps to arrive at the correct view and that is to not view people as intrinsically bad, but to see them as the result of their **causes, conditions and dependent relationships**. People are the result of their past actions, upbringing, parental guidance, environment, culture, teachers' influence, childhood experiences, sibling rivalries, intelligence, health etc.

I know Nick very well and am aware of his background. However, to discuss anything personal is beyond the scope of this book and is contrary to my current practices. It suffices to say that if I had had exactly the same background and upbringing, then I may well have turned out exactly the same and acted similarly. I will say more about this subject later when I describe the events in 2002 when I was mugged by a group of Somali refugees.

When we do explore the causes, conditions and dependent relationships that cause actions and their effects, then we usually find that "aggressor" and "victim" disappear. This will make the mind calm, peaceful and balanced. This balanced mind, free from attachment and aversion, can be described as a state of **equanimity**, which in turn can provide the foundation for forgiveness and cherishing others.

Another excellent practice is to **separate the person** (e.g. Nick) **from his actions**. The person is not intrinsically bad; it is the action that may be wrong. This is similar to telling a child that his or her actions were incorrect, rather than telling the child he or she is bad. In a similar way we all have times when we act incorrectly, so we in turn need to forgive others.

I can see that Olivia, like me, had endured a lot of hurt and suffering. Consequently, I have never judged or criticised her in any way. Unfortunately, in the past, I have born a lot of animosity towards Nick. I believed he acted purely out of self interest and betrayed me in an underhand and treacherous way, causing a great deal of harm and pain. In this respect he is my greatest teacher, has pointed out my weaknesses and has constantly provided me with my most beneficial lessons for progress.

Geshe Langri Tangpa in the fifth verse of the "Eight Verses for Training the Mind" says:

"Even if someone I have helped,
And of whom I had great hopes,
Nevertheless harms me without reason,
May I see him as my holy Spiritual Guide"

If indeed, I can see Nick as my kind teacher, I will have achieved the most beneficial mind for myself and others. Nick has pointed out my biggest weaknesses. I now need to continue to work on correcting them.

Unless I have someone to betray me, or harm me without reason, how will I learn to forgive and not harbour resentment? Not forgiving is like taking poison and expecting the other person to be harmed or die.

Similarly, wishing harm on those who have hurt you, causes most harm to yourself. I needed to learn to let go of all resentment. In this respect I need to consider Nick to be very kind in providing these lessons.

In Merchant of Venice, Shakespeare talks about mercy blessing both the giver and receiver. So it is with forgiveness. The correct view, as in the context of (Buddha's) wisdom, is always the most beneficial view and the one that leaves the "victim" with a calm, peaceful mind. The "aggressor" will also then benefit.

I should be able to forget what has happened and my opinion of what is right or wrong. After all it is only my opinion and will be formed purely from the reference point of myself. Others will have a different opinion of what is correct, so why should I insist my view is right?

I don't think it's a co-incidence that at the very end of what some consider to be Shakespeare's final play before retirement, he deals with reconciliation and forgiveness. In The Tempest, Prospero remembers the evil of Alonso, Antonio and Sebastian but forgives them. The relevant quote is below:

> *"Though with their high wrongs I am struck*
> *to the quick,*
> *Yet with my nobler reason 'gainst my fury*
> *Do I take part: the rarer action is*
> *In virtue than in vengeance: they being penitent,*
> *The sole drift of my purpose doth extend*
> *Not a frown further."*

The final words of The Tempest epilogue, again spoken by Prospero about mercy are:

> *"As you from crimes would pardon'd be,*
> *Let your indulgence set me free."*

If I wish to continue to develop, then I must learn to forgive and respect Nick as I should all other people.

Pride can also be a hindrance to progress and a proud mind will also convince anyone they are correct. Pride always leads to a fall and will cause suffering. Consequently, I need to practise **humility**, the opponent of pride. Humility is a virtuous mind that will help avoid suffering. Basically, to be happy, I need to practise **not taking myself too seriously**.

Humility also helps provide the foundations to aid the transition from cherishing self to cherishing others. Without humility it is difficult not to be obsessed by oneself, thus wallowing in a prison of problems, difficulties and suffering.

Buddhist master and Bodhisattva Shantideva teaches that it is the wish to be happy that causes us to be unhappy. Being obsessed with our own happiness, freedom and desires, is the cause of all conflict in the world. **Cherishing others** is the source of all happiness. These are big lessons to learn and understand. Fortunately, I would soon embark on this journey.

If you truly cherish another then there is no foundation for the negative, destructive minds such as hatred, anger and jealousy. It is these negative minds that cause our suffering.

Geshe Langri Tangpa in the second verse of the "Eight Verses for Training the Mind" says:

> *"Whenever I associate with others,*
> *May I view myself as the lowest of all,*
> *And with a perfect intention,*
> *May **I Cherish Others as Supreme**".*

If I practise humility, to dispel pride and an overstated feeling of self importance, I will then have room to be able to cherish others. By cherishing others and Nick in particular, there will be no foundations for hostility and/or resentment. Similarly any suffering will cease.

Writing these sections has brought to the surface all the old feelings of hurt. I still have a long way to go with my practices, but Nick has provided me with opportunities for development and a barometer for how successful I am. I know my pursuit of continuous improvement requires a lot more hard work.

Suffering can actually provide opportunities. At this point my suffering had provided a platform by which I had achieved financial security and reasonable career progress. These achievements would pale into insignificance, with other lessons I was about to learn through a monumental change in my life, goals, philosophies and my personal spiritual "journey". I was about to make the transition from ambition to purpose and meaning, from materialism to spirituality, from the pursuit of success to the practice of **contentment**.

A New Romance

I had been with Sally for five and a half years. After splitting up, Roger, a friend from my tennis club, told me a lady was asking about me. She was recently separated and I didn't recognise her from her maiden name. I asked Roger what she was like and he just said "beautiful".

Very soon after this chat with Roger the lady approached me and we started dating. Although we both fancied each other initially, it was soon apparent that we had very little in common. It only lasted a handful of dates. However, it was good for my confidence to have someone very attractive chase after me within a week or two of becoming single.

As a recently single man, working nearer home, I started mixing more with people from the tennis/squash club. A squash buddy Phil invited me to a number of social events with his group of friends and in September I went on a week-long holiday with them. By the end of this week I had developed a crush on one of the group, Andrea, and felt she was also interested in me. We started dating shortly after this holiday.

Andrea was attractive and intelligent, but her greatest asset was that she had a great determination to succeed at whatever she put her mind to. She was a good squash player and represented the county and would go on to play for England in her age group (over forties). Over a period of six years, we dated off and on for about two and a half years in total. She was very interested in sport, her career and business.

On our second date, Andrea gave me a psychometric "disc" test. This was a simple test designed to assess the characteristics of dominance, influencing, steadiness and compliance. It was typical of Andrea, to have fun and assess me for suitability using business and management techniques. It turned out to be predictably accurate and we scored in a similar manner for the various characteristics.

The only real difference, from what I recall, was that Andrea scored higher on "dominance", while I scored higher on "influencing". I told Cab about how similar our personalities were and he jokingly replied "I just hope you never have children!".

Andrea's whole life revolved around sport and she was on the Executive Management Committee of my tennis and squash club. This gave me a great opportunity to play a few pranks.

My squash playing friend Roger Toolc (not his real name) had once started bragging, on a lads' drinking night at the club, about how many times he had had sex on his honeymoon night. He was a bit drunk and didn't realise his wife had turned up to give him a lift home and was standing right behind him. His wife had a face like thunder and was not amused.

Andrea used to produce a newsletter for all the members (approximately 1,300). I changed the front sheet and replaced one article with a limerick about Roger. We only printed one of the altered copies and I delivered this to Roger's house. The limerick is below:

> *A club member aptly named Toole,*
> *drank beer until he talked like a fool.*
> *The stories he told,*
> *were amazing and bold.*
> *Seven times was the usual rule!*

Roger's wife Jill was horrified, as she thought all the club's membership would be seeing this version and she feared relentless leg pulling of a very personal nature. She was very relieved when she got to the club and realised the membership would be seeing the original version without the limerick.

There was also an attractive friend of mine called Jen, who had been out with quite a few of the eligible men at the club. I got hold of a club letter-heading and sent her an official looking letter, purporting to be from the Management Committee. It started off very seriously reprimanding Jen for her improper conduct with male members and seemingly trying to work her way through the entire men's squash team.

As the letter progressed the claims became increasingly ludicrous and by the final paragraph it was clear I was just pulling Jen's leg. The letter gave us a few good laughs and Jen admitted she was horrified when she had started reading the trumped up charges.

These pranks were all in good spirit and were taken as such by the victims. During this period I spent quite a bit of time socialising with people at the club as well as playing plenty of sport.

Andrea says she regards difficulties as being "character forming" challenges. In my book I refer to this as learning how to "transform adversity". I felt Andrea's determination to succeed was born from the inevitable difficulties that had come her way, as occur in all our lives. It is merely the type of difficulties that differ.

In many ways Andrea was just like me and there were similarities in the coping strategies we had developed. We all have adversity and can learn from these occurrences. Certainly in my case, I was learning from the suffering I had endured. Is our teacher always in front of us? Is suffering actually a gift?

Consequently, our personalities bore many similar characteristics. Hence Cab's light hearted comments that he hoped we would never have children together.

Andrea was probably the right partner at that time. I was still interested in sport, business and my own career, so we had sufficient in common, plus some mutual friends. However, as my interest in spirituality increased, my interest in business and career diminished. Consequently, we appeared to simply grow apart.

6

From Ambition to Purpose

I had now been a property owner for about twelve years and the mortgage on my luxury apartment was now nearly paid off. Within five years I would own another two properties, with minimal borrowings. I had been reasonably successful from a material perspective. However, I was now more aware than ever that whatever I achieved I would still not be content. Again I had performed my part of the conventional life contract, but I was wondering what was the real meaning of life and how could suffering and problems be avoided?

My personal search for happiness and contentment was intensifying. However, I simply didn't know where or how to start my journey. My mother had been meditating regularly since the 1970s. However, I didn't really know what this entailed and the family would affectionately and light heartedly refer to her as a "harmless crank".

I had been introduced to a meditation and philosophy group a few years earlier. I only heard a few teachings, but it had whetted my appetite. It was interesting, but (ironically) I assumed I would go back to it when I had more time. I was simply too busy with my career. Now business and my career were assuming less importance, so the time was right.

I joined the philosophy group at around the time I started going out with Andrea and eighteen months later I was initiated into meditation. I had now started my spiritual journey. The combination of meditation and eastern philosophies provided the support system that I had been searching for all my life.

I sometimes regretted not finding wisdom earlier, but in all probability I simply wasn't ready then. Maybe I needed to learn some life lessons first and to know true suffering. If everything in life always went perfectly we wouldn't need the support system of these philosophies or meditation. However, my life, despite moderate conventional and financial success, had not gone perfectly, so I needed both.

I would soon learn that problems did not exist externally, but existed within the mind. At the very least, it was how the mind reacted that would determine the size of any problem. I would also learn from experience, which is the only way to gain faith and validation, that problems became smaller after meditation. My first meditation teacher said "meditation will be your best friend throughout your life" and he would be proved to be correct.

I will talk in later sections in far greater detail about these philosophies, the wisdom that has helped me in my recent life and about meditation in particular. However, at this moment in my life spirituality was being dovetailed with my traditional interests i.e. sport, career and financial security.

I lapped up the philosophies about the power of the mind and how to control it to find inner peace and happiness. My greatest problems with Olivia had been the result of having an illusory mind of fear. Now I was really ready to progress fast.

At Nelson Mandela's inauguration speech he used a quote, "our greatest fear is not that we are inadequate, our greatest fear is that we are powerful beyond measure". Fear would no longer hold me back. I didn't want any self limiting beliefs to cause problems and suffering, as they had previously.

I found a lovely quote recently called "State of Mind". It said:

> *It's all in the state of the mind.*
> *If you think you are beaten, you are.*
> *If you think you dare not, you don't.*
> *If you like to win, but you think you can't, it's*
> *almost sure you won't.*
> *If you think you'll lose, you've lost.*
> *For out in the world you find success begins*
> *with a fellow's will.*
> *It's all in the State of the Mind.*

There is **nothing more powerful than Mind**. If mind tells people to kill, whether themselves or others, then they will kill. Although this is the negative side of mind, it is nevertheless very empowering to know that a positive mind can help you achieve anything you want to achieve. You are only one thought from changing the rest of your life and thoughts can be easily changed (from negative to positive).

This quote that I was "powerful beyond measure" was to become a personal mantra. I would joke about it with friends who I played sport with. However, I would also use this belief to ensure I would never again let my life be determined by fear and self limiting beliefs, regarding anything that was important to me.

If my mind believed I was powerful beyond measure, then I would be so. This isn't arrogance, it is simply self belief. We can go through the process of imagining, visualising, and believing, until we create a reality in mind.

In the same way if a child is told he/she is stupid, poor at maths or hopeless at, say, singing, this can become a belief and his/her reality. These self-limiting beliefs will then hold him/her back throughout his/her life. I'm sure we all know of instances where this has occurred.

The deep root of failures in our lives is to think, "oh how useless and powerless I am". It is essential to think strongly and forcefully, "I can do it", without boasting or fretting.

I had suffered enough through my own fear, lack of confidence and self-limiting beliefs. I didn't want to be held back any longer in any matters that were important. The loss of Olivia was the biggest example of this and I certainly didn't want anything else like it to ever occur again.

Also, we can have a great influence on others by our attitude. As Melvin, a networking friend of mine, often says **"attitude is contagious, is yours worth catching?"**. It is important to always have a happy and positive state of mind, so that you can have a positive effect on others. I call this the "ripple effect".

Have you noticed how quickly negativity can spread or how quickly people being judgmental and/or critical can influence others to act the same way? This negativity can spread from person to person like a raging fire leaping from house to house.

I have often contemplated how easily people are influenced by others and how they will take on their negativity. This occurs because people don't have virtuous minds. If they did have virtuous minds they simply wouldn't judge or criticise others and the raging fire of negativity would simply lose its power. Unable to gather momentum, it would eventually die out. In this respect we can all have a major and positive influence on the lives of family, friends and our community.

Career or Integrity?

In 1997 my nine and a half year career with the large plc was nearing an end. There were changes on the main board, which included a new Group Finance Director. The new Group FD had previously been a Divisional FD and that division had traditionally had very weak financial control. Rather than try to improve control, the division's strategy had been to merely protect themselves from head office intervention/monitoring. There was a culture of deceit, weak controls, aggression, dishonesty and cover ups.

Derek and I were unhappy with the changes and main board directors were putting pressure on us to act in ways that could have led to us compromising our professional duties. In internal audit, independence and free access to the Chairman of the Audit Committee are fundamental principles to be upheld, for the protection of the company and the shareholders' interests. However, I was threatened by a main board director with dismissal if I did speak directly to the Chairman of the Audit Committee, as was my professional right.

There were matters of great significance that needed to be brought to the attention of the Chairman of the Audit Committee (CAC). Unfortunately, this stress made Derek ill and I was left to make a stand against the Group Chief Executive Officer (CEO), to ensure we carried out our professional duties and the CAC was sufficiently aware of all relevant matters. For me this stand was career limiting, but necessary to maintain my integrity.

The Group CEO now had it in for me and I had upset a big ego. He was ready to fight dirty. However, I reasoned I was in a strong position. My executive contract required six months notice and my employers didn't want a tribunal case for wrongful dismissal, or the truth to come out and hit the national and/or financial press. As I had done previously, I decided not to profit from or exploit the situation.

I was put under extreme pressure, while also having an increased workload. Effectively I also had to perform Derek's role, without any extra pay. Meditation helped me a lot. Whenever, I was put under extreme pressure I would meditate more. Meditation provided the balance and enabled me to maintain a relatively calm, peaceful mind, which helped me to deal with all the stress. Nevertheless, it was clearly time for me to move on.

During this time I remember speaking to Mark and James, who were two Group Computer Auditors, about the power of the mind and the support and power of meditation. I got on well with them both and Mark had said that if Derek didn't return he would be happy to work for me.

I can remember the conversation leading to me saying that I didn't intend being ill again, through the power of controlling my mind and meditation. I had been a bit insensitive, as Mark's wife had a number of health issues. Mark startled me and snapped "that's a load of rubbish". However, as I write fifteen years later, I don't think I have taken any traditional medicine, apart from for a few dental problems, for twenty-five years or so. The cough I had in The Gambia in 1986, after my marathon, was probably the last time I took any.

I am a big believer that if I have a healthy mind then my body will also be healthy. The word "disease", indicates "to not be at ease". The placebo effect is a valid phenomenon, which is the result of believing one will recover. That in turn will lead to actual recovery.

This belief is similar to Buddhist tantric practices of going through the process of "imagination", "visualisation", "belief" and ending with "reality" (i.e. a positive result). In a similar way hypochondriacs and depressed people will experience more sickness than the average person. As everything starts with imagination you could say that it is the most powerful "nation".

I now keep myself very fit with sport and exercise. I have been virtually teetotal since 1987 (i.e. since I was thirty-two). I have never smoked cigarettes or taken illegal drugs (apart from one dodgy slice of cake Cab once gave me) and now live off a healthy vegetarian diet of fruit, fibre, vegetables and protein. I also "exercise" my immune system by not having any cleaning materials with toxic substances.

I have no wish to "clean myself to death". When it comes to good health, like everything else in life, I believe you make your own luck. I make affirmations that I am able to avoid all sickness and have achieved this result, as far as anyone is able to do so. I have also read on this subject as to how meditation and a healthy mind can heal the body.

So far my affirmations have resulted in a healthy body. One lady, in one of the meditation classes I run, said to me how "lucky" I was with my good health. I just replied "maybe we make our own luck".

With regard to finalising my corporate employment, I waited until I received a memo, which evidenced that I had been asked to act in an unprofessional manner. I then went to the Group Human Resources (HR) Manager and told him that I wasn't a solicitor, but I thought I had "a good case for constructive dismissal". The Group HR Manager just said "leave it with me". I assume he then spoke to the CEO.

I was offered a further two months employment, with the flexibility to look for alternative work, then my contract would be paid up and I was to be included in the next wave of head office redundancies. I was also offered my company car and laptop computer at reasonable prices. It was the least I could have expected, but I chose not to exploit the situation and I accepted their offer.

Other colleagues who were made redundant would look very worried and ask me what I would do. I would always just smile and say "anything I choose to do". I might have had a comfortable package, share options and financial security, but there were more important things to do with my life.

As Derek and I were at the end of our employment, I said to Derek "every time I have encountered aggression, we have found a cover-up of fraud or a major error/weakness". Derek just nodded and replied "yes, every time!".

Now, in business, whenever I encounter extreme staff behaviour, aggression, defensiveness or arguing against the implementation of and/or adherence to financial systems, my in-built "fraud detector" starts to become active. It is invariably correct.

My career with the family business and large plc could be summed up with the words of Desiderata. "Exercise caution in your business affairs; for the world is full of trickery. But let this not blind you to what virtue there is; many persons strive for high ideals; and everywhere life is full of heroism".

My mind was such that I saw the trickery, but not enough of the virtue, high ideals or heroism. I was changing my external world, but I also needed to work on making my mind more positive.

Pursuing New Interests and Going Green

After leaving the large plc, I had more time to pursue hobbies. I had always been interested in the environmental movement and became more involved with Greenpeace and Friends of the Earth (FOE).

Our blue planet is very beautiful and provides us with all the resources we need. If we destroy it or if some sort of massive damage occurs because of man's negligence, where do we go?

Soon I would take on a prominent role helping to lead the waste and recycling campaign in Birmingham. I had received training and experience in presentation skills in my corporate life, so I also took on responsibility for the FOE presentations in Birmingham. I would create visual aids and give presentations at schools, colleges, universities, social clubs, churches, faith centres, political party meetings, community centres etc.

I once followed on stage the television personality and scientist Brian Cox. We were talking to about two hundred school children at a science conference. It was my role to talk about the disadvantages of genetically modified food. The presentation went well.

I really enjoyed these presentations, but there were few others willing to help. People really fear talking in public, as I used to. I had now gained one of the two goals I set back in 1979 to become "confident", but I had merely managed to let go of my self-limiting beliefs, by facing my fears. I am a big advocate of the sportswear "philosopher" that says **"just do it!"**, or in other words **"face the fear and do it anyway!"**.

I had an interesting time with the campaigning and presentations for FOE. However, as my interest in meditation, philosophies and spirituality increased I started to spend less time with FOE. It was simply the way my interests were evolving and I just "moved on".

I still support the green movement's campaigning. However, this is really treating the symptoms. The real problem of overconsumption of the world's resources, and the resultant pollution, is man's greed. I now believe we need to treat this cause and I need to control my own mind before trying to convert others. In this respect a drowning man can't save another man from drowning.

One of my current maxims is "nature knows best". By looking at innocent animals, insects, ants, bees etc., it is easy to develop respect for them. They have no constitution and no police force, yet they live in harmony through the natural law of existence. However, man's unsustainable consumption of nature's resources is relentless, fuelled by short term greed.

I love the quote attributed to an ancient native American Indian chief "only when the last tree has been chopped down, only when the last fish has been caught and only when the last river has been poisoned, will man realise, he can't eat money". We only have one planet, yet we are in danger of consuming all resources within a few generations.

It is man's greed that needs to be abated. Yet self interest continues to prevail and wealthy nations will rarely agree on adequate preventative action. George Bush senior is attributed as saying "the American lifestyle is not negotiable!".

The evidence shows that man's greed and increased wealth has not led to any corresponding increase in happiness. Man's motivation, based on greed, is not sincere or virtuous. Consequently, people remain dissatisfied deep down. The way forward has to be to educate mankind as to what are the true causes of happiness.

My "campaigning" now is to try to control my own mind and help others to do the same, in the hope that inner peace can be achieved. I am now committed to the concept that outer peace can only be achieved, where there is first inner peace.

Corporate Freedom – Self Employed or Self Unemployed!

In 1998 I left employment. To be honest, I am highly independent and self employment suits me more than employment. I don't fit well into teams and am a bit of a perfectionist, setting high standards that others usually won't want to aspire to. Indeed, I now describe myself as "unemployable".

I didn't have a family to support and decided to become self employed. Because I deal with large projects, the nature of my income is "feast or famine". However, on balance I have managed to achieve a reasonable income. Andy has also now become a self employed transformer designer. He describes himself as being self employed, but sometimes "self unemployed".

He has managed to do well for himself, without having to do any advertising or marketing. He works in a small industry, where he is well known. He is also well respected and is known to be trustworthy.

Self employment provided me with a comfortable income, financial security and more importantly would enable me to devote more time to my hobbies including spiritual learning and practices. I was also free from boardroom politics, big company pressure and unethical employers.

I had gained a comfortable financial position in just twelve years since qualifying as an accountant and was now able to save and invest more. Any achievements were due to hard work, plus the financial knowledge that came with my work and accountancy training. I also used to assiduously read the Guardian money section each week. Effort is required in order to achieve anything in life. My networking friend Melvin always says **"reward only comes before work in the dictionary"**.

Apart from hard work, determination to succeed and my financial training I also put into practice two guidelines I had remembered from "A" level economics. These are the need for "risk spreading" and "buying and selling investments at the right time". I had also inherited my (accountant) father's belief that "money isn't for spending (it's for investing)!".

Risk spreading simply means not having all your eggs in one basket. My personal rule was, if one investment went bad it wouldn't account for more than say ten percent of the overall portfolio. For example I always made sure I had a balanced portfolio of investments split between property, pensions, share ISAs, cash and other managed investment funds.

Most of these investments in share ISAs and pensions would provide tax benefits and purchases would mainly be made by regular monthly payments, so that I would buy at "average" prices. If I made single payment investments then I would try to do so when the FTSE 100 index was relatively low.

Within each investment category, I would also have a number of separate investments. For example I have occupational pensions and two separate private (self employed) pension funds. Similarly, I have owned a number of investment funds and share ISA funds. Each fund in turn comprises a number of different companies' shares, some of which are UK based and some overseas etc.

The second financial "guideline" I employed, was a quote I heard in my economics class. A very wealthy and successful man said "I just **buy when everyone else sells and I sell when everyone else buys**". By this he meant that he bought when prices were low and sold investments when prices were high. I used to study and keep my eye on two key ratios, the average house price to average salary and the average FTSE 100 index P/E (price to earnings) ratio.

Most people invest using emotion not analytical criteria. For example, if house prices rocket, many people will then buy property on the basis that it appears to be a great investment. However, they are usually buying at the top of the market, with an impending crash imminent.

Traditionally average house prices should be about three and a half times average salaries, because that is what people can afford and what they can borrow. Currently in 2012, this ratio is about seven, despite record low interest rates to support (relatively) high house prices. Consequently, I wouldn't invest in new property at the moment.

In the late 1990s house prices appeared to be relatively low. However, as we approached the end of 1999 the average FTSE 100 index P/E ratio approached approx 35. This suggested a very low return (less than three per cent) on what are relatively high risk investments. The financial press were suggesting share prices would climb higher. However, I took the view that share prices were too high and started selling shares and buying more property.

I did well, perhaps not as well as I could have done, but well enough. Shortly after selling shares the FTSE 100 crashed from a high of nearly 7000 to approximately 3500. My decisions felt vindicated. However, I always felt they were low risk strategies.

Professionally, I do not give investment advice and am not authorised to do so. Consequently, I am most definitely not giving investment advice here. I am merely informing you of the strategy which I have employed in my adult life, for myself.

Through hard work and application I had done reasonably well at everything since the disaster of 1979. However, the one area where I had not been successful was in my love life and I had made the decision not to date so often and certainly not on a casual basis. I also often wondered, what had happened to Olivia?

It was clear after all these years, that Olivia would almost undoubtedly have a new life, partner(s) and possibly her own family. In the past, I had always wished for the ideal that Olivia and I would at some time be reunited. However, as each year passed this was looking less and less likely.

What was now most important was to have peace of mind and closure. At the very least, I needed Olivia to know the truth, that I had always cared for her and had never intended to hurt her in any way. When would I get the opportunity to speak openly with her and after all these years how would she respond?

The End for Fatima

In the year 2000, Fatima, our beautiful family dog, resembling a Bavarian Sheep Dog, died, at the grand old age of sixteen. She had outlived all her brothers. She had had a few health problems in the latter years. Firstly, she developed some arthritis problems. Although Fatima could still walk well, she couldn't run so fast. She also developed a growth near her neck. I suspect this may have been caused by a "medicinal" collar to prevent fleas.

Then she went deaf. Finally, near the end she suffered from kidney problems and became incontinent. The inevitable sufferings of ageing, sickness and finally death were apparent.

If anything these ailments and her ensuing vulnerability just brought us closer together. Soon after she went deaf, on one of our many walks over Clent Hills, Fatima nipped under a hedge and went into another field. I continued walking but now she couldn't hear me when I called and she got lost. She found her way home, but this was out of character as she would always want to return with me. Indeed she was waiting in the road to my mother's house for me.

On another occasion Fatima had a horse walk up behind her. She had been raised in stables and was usually very comfortable with horses around. However, now the horse could approach from behind without Fatima hearing it and she was no longer fast enough to escape.

The horse was very friendly and was nudging Fatima's backside and tail with its nose. I thought this was funny and was sure the horse was just amusing itself. However, Fatima looked me in the eyes as she tried unsuccessfully to get away and I could tell she was actually quite scared. Previously, she could always detect horses and if necessary would just nip under a hedge.

This must have been quite frightening and traumatic for Fatima. Consequently, from that moment she was very wary of horses. I can remember her later stopping at a stile while I had continued into the field. She now always looked out for horses and wouldn't enter this particular field because there were some in it. I looked at her. She looked into my eyes, then looked at the horses and back, to gesture her concerns. She was looking to me for protection and indeed was starting to depend upon me more and more. This strengthened our relationship.

In this instance I gestured for her to come to me and I then pointed to another stile about ten yards away, which would take us back home. She did as I asked and trotted towards me. Then one horse approached me. Fatima stood behind my legs and as I beckoned her to go under the other stile she did as I asked and waited for me, while I ensured the horse stopped with me and didn't chase after her. The operation was successfully completed.

Recently I saw an excellent BBC documentary about how the special relationship between dogs and humans has evolved. The documentary suggested that part of this success was the ability of dogs to communicate. This was partly with body language and tone of voice, but also dogs may have developed the bark to further improve this communication. I am convinced this is correct and the more Fatima became vulnerable and dependent upon me, the better our communication became.

Near the end Fatima's kidney condition became a serious problem. She would sometimes sit at my feet and then begin shaking uncontrollably as though in a fit. I would comfort her as much as I could, but she was in distress. Also, she needed to constantly urinate and her quality of life was becoming so poor that eventually the difficult decision was taken, in consultation with the vet, that she needed to be put to sleep.

In the last few months, I remember taking Fatima, at the ripe old age of sixteen, for a walk to the nearest fields. She loved our walks, but now as soon as we entered the first field she just stopped to relieve herself. I tried to entice her to go further by walking about fifty yards up the hill. I then turned around to see what she was doing. She was still at the bottom and just looked sadly into my eyes before she turned around and stared at the stile that we had entered the field by. She was clearly telling me she couldn't walk any further and needed to go back home.

Near the end I visited mother's house for a Sunday lunch and Fatima didn't greet me at the front door with her usual frantic, excited barking. By now she just stayed in her basket most of the time. I walked through to greet mother in the kitchen and washed my hands before lunch. I then felt something touch my leg. It was Fatima nudging the back of my knee with her nose. As I turned around she was already slowly ambling back to the comfort of her basket.

Fatima was now virtually bed, or to be more accurate basket, ridden. However, it was very touching that despite great difficulty and discomfort, she just wanted to say hello. I tried to stroke her, but she just wanted to get back to her basket. It was clear she was nearing the end.

Finally, when the difficult decision to have Fatima put down was made, I got the call from mother and took them both down to the vet. As we waited for the vet, Fatima continually needed to go out to urinate. Mother and I both went out with her and as she sat on the pavement she just looked very sadly into my eyes. I'm sure she knew it was the end.

As the vet administered the injection, I held and comforted Fatima. She trusted me implicitly, as she always had, looked me in the eyes and smiled with all her teeth bared, even as I led her to the death I believe she was expecting. She seemed to die peacefully, comforted by loved ones.

Fatima had provided me with many great memories, constant companionship and unconditional love. That day I had to fight back tears and indeed am doing the same again while writing this section some twelve years on. Mother was also in tears at the time of the death. Fatima had been a great companion for her especially after my father had died.

I hope when I have my own dog, in the not too distant future, that she is as good a companion as Fatima, but that is asking a lot. Fatima was exceptional.

After Fatima died we found out that she had a regular daily routine of walking to selective neighbours who she knew would give her food. She certainly liked her food and always lived up to the name "Fatty". Although she was never significantly over weight, she should have been.

I was also beginning to change a lot. I was getting more in touch with my emotions and wasn't afraid to cry. Isn't this just nature's way to wash away the hurt? As a young man I'd always just suppressed hurt. Now I was beginning to let go of hurt, to deal with it while it is current and not to allow it to grow and become suppressed in my mind, causing on-going suffering.

By now when I meditated, particularly after a stressful period, I would often be aware of tears running down my cheeks. This was never painful and indeed felt good. I now consider this to be a release of tension and a very beneficial

7

The New Millennium
and a New Direction

I gained an incredible amount from meditation and my meditation group. However, after five years I started to feel that I had heard the most profound teachings and the classes for the last eighteen months or so had lacked any more profundity.

I was reading extensively for my personal development. At first I read self development books and conventional psychology books, including some about transactional analysis. It was all interesting and it had whetted my appetite. Now, with the meditation group I had started reading about and studying other philosophies and faiths such as Taoism, Hinduism and Buddhism.

I wanted to explore other areas of spirituality, so I left the meditation school, but continued to meditate for an hour a day. I found their advice to meditate for two thirty minute sessions in the morning and evening to be invaluable. I could prove this from my own experience. If ever I missed a session, the difference in my ability to remain calm and peaceful suffered significantly. Life was simply not so good.

The profound concentration of meditation results in Inner Peace. In turn **Inner Peace is a necessary condition for Happiness.** Without concentration **the mind is weak.** Again,

I could prove this from my own experience. There were many situations where my external conditions were perfect. However, if my mind was disturbed and negative, such as if I dwelt on a (perceived) problem, then happiness would be impossible.

I was learning that if I could maintain a calm and peaceful mind at all times, I would not experience any problems. Too frequently we blame the external situation for our problems and unhappiness. However, problems only occur when the mind is negative. If the mind remains positive, whatever the situation, then we will not experience any problems.

Similarly, our energy is where our thoughts are. If you dwell on problems, hurt or pain, then you will give them power. On the other hand if you concentrate on something neutral, such as the breath, or something virtuous, then the problem, hurt or pain will simply not exist. A virtuous mind will always be calm, peaceful and relaxed. It will also be free from stress, agitation and problems.

Again the words of Desiderata are very relevant: "Go placidly amid the noise & haste, & remember what peace there may be in silence".

Once you have discovered the power and benefits of meditation there is no going back. At the time of writing, I am in my seventeenth year of meditating for an hour a day. I would say I have been about ninety percent effective in achieving this objective and the results have been immense. I am sure I will continue doing this for the rest of my life. Why wouldn't I do so?

For two years I continued my reading of eastern philosophies. I also practised tai chi and chi gong, attended a number of spiritual workshops and travelled to a number of spiritual "retreats" abroad in Egypt, Israel, France and Spain. All this led me to make some more good friends in Andy and Ian, who I nicknamed the "Dirty Vicar" and "Dirty Plumber" respectively.

Andy had a fantastic loud "dirty" laugh and was a great foil for my jokes. He also looked like a vicar and had a "friar" hair cut. It wasn't long before Andy's nickname became widely popular and even one of the spiritual teachers called him "Bishop" or "Bish". Ian and Andy remained friends for many years.

I learned a lot from all of these courses and trips. However, they were very much like holidays. Although they were very enjoyable, often in beautiful, exotic and interesting places, I felt I needed more profound study. I'm sure they fulfilled a need for that time, if only to let me know that I was ready for something more "pure" and "authentic". Indeed it was while on one of these trips abroad that I bought and read avidly two books by a Buddhist teacher.

I now had my spiritual focus and wanted to study more about Buddha's teachings.

Good Company (2002)

I felt what these spiritual trips and courses lacked was continuity and constancy. My first meditation and philosophy group had regular weekly classes. In addition I was asked to give a further night each week in service for others. This service included assisting teachers and some teaching myself. With the same group, I had also started studying Shakespeare and learning the ancient language Sanskrit on a Saturday morning. Consequently, I had the constant reminders necessary to maintain a relatively calm and peaceful mind.

My spiritual trips and courses were sporadic. The leader of the philosophy and meditation school warned me, when I left, that I would miss the **"Good Company"** required to progress and develop. He was absolutely right, but I wanted to do things my way. I would learn these lessons the hard way and my "teacher" would continue to present all necessary guidance along the way.

Immediately after leaving the meditation "school" I joined one of my long standing friend Andy's social clubs. I thought I could combine spirituality with excitement and more socialising. It was a club of middle aged people. I was forty-six and in this age group must have been considered to be an eligible male.

Immediately, one of the female members invited me out. I didn't see her as a potential partner, but thought I'd be able to enjoy the evening and her company. We had an enjoyable meal and a few days later went to another event. It turned into a bit of a nightmare. On the second occasion, although I didn't drink, she got quite drunk and tried very hard to get me to have sex with her.

I now have a personal code of conduct to avoid unnecessary hurt to others and I won't have sex unless I see someone as a potential long term partner. I managed to successfully extricate myself from this situation. The lady seemed to respect my position and how I had dealt with the matter. However, from this moment she started to follow me around. At club events she would often get drunk and would be a nuisance constantly questioning why I wouldn't go out with her and trying to find inconsistencies with things I had said. She simply wouldn't take no for an answer.

If any woman wants to impress me, then getting drunk and following me everywhere is not the way to do it. This particular woman would then start talking to all the other women, sometimes building me up and on other occasions being very critical. This led to a lot of gossip and negativity spread quickly, making life unpleasant.

I was already pondering that I did indeed need "good company". However, things were about to get much worse.

Karen an ex girlfriend of Andy's was having some problems. She was giving up university and intended returning to the Midlands. I agreed to let her stay in my empty one bedroom apartment for a nominal rent. Karen was also a member of Andy's social club.

Karen had a history of falling out with people and causing significant problems for all those involved, even if they had tried to help her. However, I was confident I would be able to cope with anything that arose.

I told Karen that I was looking to sell the apartment in the near future and offered her a very reasonable price if she wanted it. Karen often told me how much she liked the apartment, but also gave many reasons why it wasn't suitable for her. Karen never made any offer.

In early 2002, the fears after the USA "9/11" incident subsided and the housing market in Britain started to really take off. The terrorist atrocity had lowered confidence and created a suppressed housing market, but now the lid was off. I kept Karen informed of all the interest.

When I told her I had received an acceptable offer she visited me and said "I will make the same offer, but not give you a penny more". The value had moved up further, but I chose not to gazump anyone. I informed Karen that I would be accepting the offer from the other party, as was my right. I felt I had already committed to the other person and I don't break my word.

Unfortunately, Karen reacted very badly and said I was going to cause her immense problems for some months. She then went into a dark and depressed mood. Actually, she chose to inflict this pain upon herself. She was in the negative world of blame, judgment and denial. It was all her own doing, but she was determined to make my life as difficult as possible.

It was interesting to watch someone give themselves so many problems, but it was also distressing. I felt sorry for Karen who had a history of falling out with people whom she felt had harmed her, before putting great energy into seeking and trying to exact her revenge. At the end of the day, she was just harming herself and creating her own unhappiness.

Unfortunately, she did make my life difficult. Karen was quite poisonous in her comments about me and the negativity spread throughout our social club, especially amongst the ladies. This was just a social club and unfortunately there were no common values. Karen was quite vindictive and manipulative. She was also very good at it. She had had a lot of practice.

In the spring of 2002 I told Andy I would be leaving his social club. There were a lot of good people in it. Unfortunately, there was quite a lot of acrimony directed at me and I had had enough. I didn't mean anyone any harm. However, the social events were ceasing to be fun and the hassle I received was becoming frequent.

It was yet another example of how rapidly negativity can spread from one person to another without any justification and just how easily people take on the (negative) emotions of others. Again, the truth doesn't matter and the default setting for most people is negativity.

The leader of my meditation group was right. I needed Good Company and people around me who would provide support for my spiritual journey. As soon as I left the group, to pursue worldly pleasures, I encountered problems and difficulties. Chasing and desiring worldly pleasures is deceptive. It's like eating honey off a razor blade. **All sources of pleasure are also causes of suffering.** My life experiences have proven this to be true.

210

To continue to progress I needed to constantly follow a great teacher such as Christ, Buddha, Mohammed or a (Hindu) Shankaracharya. I also needed the constant exposure to their wisdom teachings and Good Company. Basically, I needed to always be **going for Refuge** in a great teacher and to have access to his/her wisdom, plus a support system. To be free from suffering is like saying, to be free from disease we need a good doctor (teacher), effective medicine (wisdom) and good nurses providing a support system (good company).

Buddhist Master Atisha said about **Good Company** "Avoid friends who cause you to increase delusions (such as anger, hatred, resentment, jealousy, and pride), and rely upon those who increase your virtue". This is similar to the words of Desiderata "Avoid loud and aggressive persons, they are vexations to the spirit".

I needed to find good company again.

My Teacher is Always in Front of me

2002 provided a number of big events and many lessons. Firstly there was the lesson about the need for Refuge and Good Company. Then, just before I left the social group, I was mugged. Finally, I also met a lovely, gorgeous lady and started dating again.

One Wednesday, I was walking back from an event with the social club in the centre of Birmingham when I passed the Hall of Memory at one end of Broad Street, where all the clubs and bars are. It was quiet except for two black men. As I got near them the one shouted "Oy, have you got a fag?".

The tone seemed hostile and I didn't recognise the accent. It wasn't a local accent, nor was it West Indian. I guessed the accents were African. I said "no" and started to quicken my step to get away. Then they ran towards me and one started pushing me from behind, saying "don't ignore my friend". He pushed me towards a wall. I stumbled towards it and turned around to face them.

Then a third person appeared from behind the wall and grabbed me around my neck. I was now trapped by the three men and they started intimidating me. One kept shouting at me while punching and hitting me, while his accomplice started going through my pockets.

They ripped and ruined my jacket. I also received a lump under my chin and a few facial bruises. It was scary, but fortunately, I was able to think clearly throughout the ordeal. Feelings of fear, hate, anger and doubt are not only painful, but keep the brain from functioning properly. This was a time for **reason not emotion**. Reason and emotion are effectively mutually exclusive.

I have heard of many instances where people have gone after threatening gangs and ended up dead or badly beaten. I reasoned that it was pointless to fight back. There were three of them and one of me. Also, they were probably street wise and knew how to fight. I hadn't been in a fight since junior school and would be no match for them.

I also reasoned that if I hurt one of them, such as by kicking them between the legs, then they would just get angry and might hurt me more. Worse still they might pull a knife or gun. Also, I often quote Kipling about the need for keeping your head while all those around you lose theirs. There is no point in being a dead hero.

I reasoned and hoped that they were just after my money, so I grabbed my wallet and threw it as far as I could. I managed to throw it approximately twenty yards. The three men then just let go of me and ran after my wallet. They picked it up and ran off laughing. It had just been a bit of fun for them and they had been successful.

I think I lost about thirty pounds in cash, but I reasoned it was the best thirty pounds I had ever spent. I also had the nuisance late at night of having to cancel all my credit cards, inform the police and make a statement. However, I was relieved that I had escaped with just minor injuries.

I also reflected that I was surprised just how calm I had remained and how this had probably helped me. I'm sure that, six years of meditating for an hour a day must have been a great benefit.

The police informed me that there had been a gang of about eleven Somali refugees who had been involved with about eight mugging incidents. On three occasions they had threatened their victims with a knife. I had been "lucky", but maybe I had made my own luck by remaining calm.

This event provided a barometer of my spiritual progress and development. I was very pleased that I had remained so calm. I was also very pleased that I didn't judge the "aggressors", nor did I bear them any animosity. However, I was also aware that my feelings towards them were neutral and that I didn't cherish or love them, as is required to attain advanced beneficial states, such as the ultimate goal of enlightenment.

I had made progress. However, I still had a long way to go. It is worth commenting that although it is important to have love and compassion for everyone, wisdom still necessitates taking the necessary action. In this case the police needed to be informed, so that they could help protect other members of the public and prevent the "aggressors" from committing further crimes. This is also for the benefit of the perpetrators of the crime.

Although I bore the "aggressors" no malice and didn't judge them, I was amazed at the reaction of others when I related the story. Perfectly reasonable people would become very judgmental and critical, often advocating a totally disproportionate response or punishment.

I remember my father often commenting about the need for fairness with disadvantaged people. He would often say that if I had been born with their parents, in a poor area, with hardly any education and no good role models or hope, then I would probably be just like them. In other words, **"never judge a man until you have walked a mile in his moccasins"**.

The words of Desiderata are always worth bearing in mind, "If you compare yourself with others, you may become vain & bitter; for always there will be greater and lesser persons than yourself".

These "criminals" had come from Somalia where there is little law or order, where criminal gangs are in control, where it's "dog eat dog", where crime is probably a necessary survival strategy and where "only the strong survive". They then travelled to Britain where they see affluent people with everything they desire. It is no wonder that they turn to crime.

When we do explore the causes, conditions and dependent relationships, which cause actions and their effects, then we usually find that labels such as "aggressor" and "victim" disappear. This is a necessary process to create the most beneficial mind for everyone. As Shakespeare said, mercy blesses both the giver and the receiver.

Altogether a very interesting experience and one that provided many lessons and a barometer for my progress!

Love at Last - but would it Last?

During the last twelve years I have had just three girlfriends/partners and in 2002 I met Carol, of whom I became very fond.

I started spending more time in my Birmingham city centre apartment, as it was handy for business and I joined the local gym. Carol was the aqua aerobics instructor there and I noticed her when I had an early morning swim before work. She would come to the pool looking absolutely gorgeous. She was very slim, but filled her swimsuit very well, with a great figure.

If Olivia was my Kim Basinger then Carol was my Sienna Miller, or at least that's how I regarded her. She had long reddish brown hair and a few freckles. It is a look I have always found attractive and Carol looked rather like Pam at the same age.

I started chatting to Carol whenever I could and although she often mentioned her daughter, she never talked about a husband or partner. She was intelligent and articulate. We had interests in common and she was concerned about the environment. I soon learned that she had split up with her husband and I was very interested.

One day I met Carol in the lounge and we shared a coffee and got on well, so I asked her if she fancied going for a pizza and/or to see a film together. Her response surprised me, she just said demonstratively "oh not while I've got all this rubbish going on in my life", referring to the split from her husband. I was surprised by her negative response, but left with my tail between my legs, thinking she wasn't interested in me after all.

Apparently, as soon as I had left Carol wondered to herself why she had responded the way she had, as she had also fancied me. She then talked about the situation with a female friend who knew me, and they tried unsuccessfully to find out my telephone number, so that she could call me. I then noticed I kept bumping into Carol and her friend Marie. Maybe all wasn't lost after all.

Soon afterwards it was my birthday. I must have mentioned this to Carol, because she bought me a small present. I was very pleased and offered to take her out for a meal to thank her. We were now an item.

Earlier in the year I had sold my first apartment. I now had less client work and plenty of spare time, so I had booked a holiday every month for six months. There was a Chi Gong week, (vegetarian) cycling holidays and spiritual trips to France (Cathar country) and Israel. I now also had a beautiful, intelligent, caring, thirty-two year old girlfriend. Life seemed to be perfect, or so I thought.

Although I was fourteen years older than Carol, she made it clear from the start that she was very fond of me. It takes me a bit longer, but I was really falling for her as well. The only problem with Carol was that she was very low on confidence and I was used to very confident ladies. She also had a very controlling ex husband.

When we first started going out, I told Carol that I hadn't had a girlfriend for two and half years and that I didn't date unless I was thinking of the lady as a potential long term partner. However, she didn't believe me and just said "men don't act like that". I mistakenly thought this wasn't a problem and that she would learn to trust me with time. Unfortunately, I was wrong.

Carol once told me a story about how, as a young girl, she had returned home from school and excitedly told her mother "mom, I'm in the nativity play". Her mother had apparently replied "why would you want to do that, you'll only make a fool of yourself". I thought this was very sad for a young girl to be put down like this and I could understand how a child would be affected and how she could easily grow up lacking confidence as a direct result of such occurrences.

I can remember once saying to Carol that I thought she was really beautiful and I meant it. She sat there pan faced and just replied "I don't feel beautiful". It was quite sad to hear this.

This was another example of how a child or person can go through the process of imagining, and visualising something until it becomes a belief and ultimately creates their reality. In this case by constantly telling a beautiful, intelligent, sensitive child she is hopeless it became a reality, resulting in very low confidence and self esteem.

When we started going out, Carol said that it was ok to keep in touch with my female friends, as she had male friends she kept in touch with. In our four months together I saw four different female friends on four occasions in total, but I was totally happy with Carol as a partner and certainly wasn't looking for anyone else.

Unfortunately, Carol did become apprehensive whenever I would meet a female friend, even if they were in a stable relationship. If I had known how nervous this made her feel, then I wouldn't have done it.

When Carol and I started going out I had already booked my holidays. However, when I returned from the holiday in France, I told her I wouldn't be booking on any more holidays without discussing matters with her. I then asked her if she wanted to go with me to France the following year. I fully intended to pay for us both. I was now smitten and assumed she was as well and that we could start to plan our lives, or at least the foreseeable future, together.

The many holidays that year also taught me that, although thoroughly enjoyable, they weren't causes of happiness in themselves. I was getting more satisfaction from Carol's company and our love life. Indeed I was returning from holidays with a longing for Carol. She was far more important than any material possessions and I was now thinking long term.

Then, in the two weeks or so before my pre-planned trip to Israel Carol's mood changed considerably. We didn't see so much of one another. She had become withdrawn and was acting strangely. I wasn't sure what the problem was, but I never thought it could be us, as I considered everything to be going perfectly. Carol was being a bit evasive, so I simply didn't get the opportunity to sort things out.

I took the view that I would sort out whatever difficulties there were upon my return from the holiday. Hopefully, the problems and mood swings were purely in the mind and would disappear anyway, rather like clouds drifting away in the sky. Unfortunately, when I did return from Israel, Carol told me that she "didn't want to be in a relationship any more". This was another bombshell and again I was badly hurt.

I asked Carol what the problem was because we didn't disagree on anything. She just said, "Only one thing, all this positive thinking". She would sometimes refer to "positive thinking" as "pop psychology". It is a shame but she wanted to wallow in self pity, living in a world of blame, denial and excuses. In this one respect we were now different. Maybe she was like I was in my teens and early twenties.

I talked to Carol's friends whenever possible, to try to resolve things. However, she had made her mind up some time ago that she wanted to split and now we were "too far down the road". It was clear that she had already put herself through a lot of pain in coming to this decision and now it was my turn to be hurt (again).

One of Carol's friends said "when she is on a downer, she just drops everyone". This had happened to me, when she started to get down. However, I can relate to it as, when problems occur, I often wish to go through life on my own. I also know other people who will quickly go to the "sanctuary" of being single, rather than face any pain that a relationship might inflict.

Another thing Carol told a friend about me was "I think he's really good looking, he's very well educated and has lots of friends, but I don't feel comfortable with all that". What a pity!

It looked like I was always going to struggle to be a part of Carol's world. However, I will always reflect on a lovely time with a beautiful, caring and intelligent lady.

Carol had also told a female friend that she thought I had been chasing other women. This simply wasn't true, as she was all I had wanted. It was also completely out of character for me to have acted this way. I reasoned that this came from her belief that she wasn't good enough and so I must be interested in women, whom, she thought, would be better than her. It was a great pity and is an example of the destructive power that self limiting beliefs can have. Unfortunately, this low self esteem was Carol's reality.

I really enjoyed my time with Carol, but it was an example of how everything in mind is mere appearance (illusion). Everything in **mind is just an illusion** and **we create our own version of reality**. It is actually quite liberating to be able to view negative states of mind and problems in this way. I believe Christ said, as a person thinks in his heart, so is he.

"Why do optimists have all the good luck?". It is important to always focus on positivity. Recently I have started carrying a "gratitude" card with me at all times. I put it in my pocket when I dress and take it out at night. It is a reminder of all the things I have to be grateful for. It puts me in a positive frame of mind. With a positive, calm, peaceful mind, problems always appear to be smaller and it helps me avoid dwelling on them to give them any power.

Carol is one of the loveliest people I have known. However, she is also one of the people most affected by negative thinking and has various health problems. I'm sure this isn't a coincidence as I believe a healthy, positive mind will result in a healthy body.

Ironically, just as twenty odd years earlier, my lack of confidence had ruined my hope of reconciliation with Olivia, now Carol's lack of confidence had ruined our relationship. Similarly, just as Olivia and I had a view of reality that was mistaken, so had Carol. All these mistaken views of reality had had a devastating, damaging and painful effect on our lives.

After Carol a number of women showed an interest in going out with me. This was very flattering, but at this time, I was only interested in Carol.

So ended another chapter in my love life.

It would be six years before my next girlfriend.

School Reunion (2002)

While I was going out with Carol, in the summer of 2002, we had a school reunion. It was nearly thirty years after we had completed our "A" levels and had left the sixth form. Ben, Gaz and Andy were there and there was a really great turnout from our class, with approximately half attending. It was interesting to see everyone again and to see how they had all fared since leaving school.

At school, I had always struggled in the top class. Consequently, I had lacked confidence and didn't think I was bright enough or physically strong enough to make a great success of my life.

Our English teacher "Tosh" was also there. I always felt that Tosh didn't like me, because I wasn't going to study the classics or go to a top university. He seemed to favour the intellectual elite and even told Gaz's parents at a parents evening that Gaz needed to get away from me. To their credit Gaz's parents had supported me. Gaz was more intelligent than me, however he probably worked less hard than I did.

After leaving school I had often thought that I'd like to go back and tell Tosh and a few other teachers, that I was now a Chartered Certified Accountant, had a Marketing Diploma and had had a successful career in business. My pride had been hurt and I wanted to go back and say "up yours, I've been a success despite what you thought!". However, now it simply didn't matter. I just saw some sad old teachers, whose pride and need to satisfy their self esteem and to feel superior had probably caused them suffering.

The most interesting observation was with my peers. I had kept myself in good physical condition and was still very fit. The contrast was startling; I now had no cause to feel inferior. I was now as athletic and strong as most of those in my class, if not more so.

More surprising was that in my career, through sheer hard work, determination and persistence, I had done as well as most of my peers and had outperformed many. My teachers had led me to believe that the intellectual elite would be running the country. I wasn't a part of the intellectual elite, but as a result of hard work and determination I had performed well. Indeed there were peers who were unemployed, with specialist skills, who seemed to have little chance of finding work.

I am now quite critical of the school system that places too much emphasis on purely academic subjects and favours those children with high IQ. Research shows it is actually those children with the highest emotional intelligence (EQ) that are successful, and frequently those with the highest IQ end up working for those with the highest EQ. Those with the highest IQ often become "boffins" and "technicians", but aren't necessarily leaders and often don't push themselves as those with high EQ do.

At school there seemed to be no recognition that children with good EQ, but moderate or low IQ, still had a great deal to offer. More importantly at school little had been done to provide basic life skills. I found this out at my cost. Through hard work I got the qualifications. However, in my twenties I simply had no idea how to cope with the inevitable problems that would come my way. In this respect we are simply thrown into life's deep end and left to sink or swim. Unfortunately, many sink with little help.

I often tell people that I had "an excellent education". I usually then add, "but it took me years to get over it". Academic subjects like geography, history, physics and chemistry have their uses. However, I believe there needs to be a balance, so that children are prepared for life.

One of the school bullies, Ted, was also at the reunion. He and his friend Jed were the fearsome "mafia" of our year. Every day they would walk up to the front of the dinner queue and push in. No one dared to argue with them. One of my class mates saw Ted, laughed and said I can remember when at school he smacked me in the face (for little or no reason). Ted was now no bigger than me and was very drunk. He was making a fool of himself and was no longer frightening. He now looked a sad figure.

This provides a good lesson that **aggressive people are invariably suffering** and have probably had a difficult life. To be able to see people this way helps ensure we **don't judge or criticise** and also helps develop **a happier and more compassionate mind**.

Buddha taught that it is easy to see the faults in others, but it is a wise man who can see the faults in himself. I would add that it is a wise man indeed who can correct all his faults, but this is the road to a happier life for everyone. Certainly, we need to concentrate on controlling and purifying our own minds first.

This school reunion was another reminder that what was in my mind was just **perception and illusion, not reality**. At school I grew up believing I was small, weedy, unattractive and not intelligent enough to be very successful. In turn I believed this would make attaining happiness difficult. However, the reality is that we can all achieve a great deal, with a powerful and positive mind.

Networking rather than Not Working (2003)

Shortly after splitting up with Carol, I met up again with some friends from the 1970s Dave "Sniffer" and Buck. Dave was nicknamed "Sniffer" (after the Leeds United goal scoring legend Alan "Sniffer" Clarke) when he scored a hat trick in one of our football matches. Dave was now a retired bank manager and Buck had his own small stationery and packaging business.

My own business as a Freelance Financial Controller or Part Time Finance Director was going through a quiet spell. Buck was a member of the world's biggest business referral organisation and he invited me to one of the weekly breakfast meetings. I was very impressed and saw this as an ideal way to make business contacts and to gain referrals.

I was also very impressed with the organisation's "givers gain" philosophy. This seemed like a great way to get hard-nosed businessmen to think of others. It fitted in with my business and spiritual values; indeed the Buddha says **"giving creates the causes for future wealth"**.

I joined the referral organisation as soon as I finished the temporary project I was working on. Like everything else I put a lot of hard work and determination into obtaining referrals and soaked up the knowledge from the training. Soon I gained a reputation as a good networker and someone with a lot of contacts.

After about nine months I was asked to become an Assistant Director (AD). This provided me with an excellent training in presentation, referral and networking skills. In turn I was responsible for training new members.

Another role I performed was to launch new "chapters" of businessmen. I reckoned I could do this whenever my own business was quiet. This would smooth out the "feast or famine" nature of being self employed. It seemed to be the ideal way to market my business, gain new skills and provide more income.

I was a member of the referral organisation for about five and a half years, of which four years were in the role of AD. As well as new skills it provided me with a lot of excellent contacts, a reasonable level of additional income and some good friends.

Networking is very powerful and it is now how I get virtually all my business. Apparently, we are just two handshakes from the Queen and six handshakes from everyone in the world. On average we have a thousand contacts each. In business, it's just a question of knowing how to use your contacts for your mutual benefit.

To give you an idea of the power of networking, around this time a friend Brian, who I had met on a cycling holiday in Eire contacted me. Brian was a walking encyclopaedia of football knowledge and he had recently been in a pub in London, when a lady started talking about a middle aged man she met on a vegetarian cycling holiday, who wore a Baggies shirt on the final day, before rushing off to see the first match of the new Premiership season. Brian knew there was only one person it could be.

The greatest provider of quality referrals to me was from a lovely lady called Sarah. Sarah joined soon after me and was a natural networker. She is very attractive, gregarious, totally honest and has a lovely "giving" nature. As a result people like her and she proved to be very good at developing business relationships and trust.

My business and skills are not easily understood by most micro business owners. Consequently, most referral group members I met went through the motions, but in their minds thought they wouldn't be able to help me or couldn't do so. Sarah was probably the only member, who would continually tell me that I was very difficult to find a referral for. This was great, she actually wanted to help, so I was able to meet her and educate her about how to get me referrals.

Sarah is my website designer and didn't come from a financial background. However, she has provided me with more referral income than anyone else. In turn she has also done a great job designing my website, which gave me credibility and has helped me gain further business.

I have managed to provide some very good referrals during my networking career. However, I remain indebted to Sarah. Sarah just wants to give; in turn she does receive a lot of referrals from numerous sources.

She has become a valued friend and provides a number of lessons. Some of her natural qualities are things I have to work at. Her best qualities as a networker are as an unconditional **Giver, someone who always respects and likes others, while not judging or criticising**.

The Nifty Fifties (2004)

In 2004 it was my fiftieth birthday and I had parties on the Friday in the grounds of my home and again at my sports club on the Saturday. This was typical of my wish to socialise and create excitement. However, excitement only creates a temporary reduction in suffering and is usually followed by despondency or a "downer".

Shortly before the partying I met up with Gaz and his wife Ann for a meal. It was just after Gaz's fiftieth and we hadn't met up for a while. It was a lovely occasion.

I hadn't been able to talk about the painful events with Olivia and "that party" for about twenty years. However, I was now ready and I wanted all my close friends to know the truth. They were genuinely concerned for me when I told them that I had been telling another lady I didn't want to dance with her, that Olivia had got very upset, that I'd been whisked away (or thrown out) and that I'd then heard she was fooling around with one of my best friends.

Gaz and Ann knew how close Olivia and I were and Ann always said that she was sure we'd get back together. Then later in the evening Gaz said "I hear you don't see Nick any more, something about him stealing a girlfriend off you". I explained that it was Olivia who they were referring to and that Nick hadn't stolen a girlfriend, but had exploited the situation, for little reward. Gaz and Ann were appalled. I just said that I didn't want to go down the negativity route.

Gaz would have been told this story by Ben, whom he saw regularly at pub quizzes. However, I noted that Ben had never told Gaz that it was about Olivia. I assumed that Ben was covering for his friend Nick, to avoid him being condemned, had the truth been known.

Gaz said something about, "well these things would have probably happened anyway". I just commented that I never had a problem with Olivia. Indeed I trusted her completely and would still do so. I'm sure Olivia was just badly hurt, although unnecessarily so and was in need of company.

Unbeknown to me at the time, this was to be the last occasion Gaz and I went out together.

The Power of Love and Truth (c2005)

Life was now much easier. While on my spiritual journey I had set one "massive goal". That was to resolve all issues in my life. The big issue, of course, was to resolve all problems with Olivia. I didn't want any negativity, hurt or suffering to remain in the minds of either of us. I hadn't seen her for about twenty-five years. Maybe I hadn't been ready, but now I was.

I went with a business contact and friend Melvin to see the inspirational David Hyner talk about setting "massive goals". There were probably about forty to fifty people there. David asked who had set massive goals and I told him what mine was. "Put your hands together for this man" said David, "he has balls of steel". I had come a long way from the young man who was once desperately lacking confidence and full of fear.

I was now gaining a reputation as a good networker. I also started, organised and managed networking groups for businessmen. My record in introducing other businessmen to my groups was very good. Most people in the groups had self-limiting beliefs that they simply weren't able to do this. They had "I can't" in their minds not "I can".

My own Independent Financial Advisor (IFA) once remarked on my achievements and said "you have no fear". I realised I had come a long way from the young man in 1978 and 1979 who was paralysed by fear and lost the person he held most dear (Olivia) as a result.

Soon afterwards, I met up with a spiritual teacher. He talked about progress and said it was now time for me to let go of "all emotional attachments". He was talking about Olivia and I was now ready.

About two weeks later I pulled into a petrol station and Olivia was there. Was this a coincidence? Is there such a thing as coincidence?

It was the first time I'd seen Olivia to talk to since 1980. I called her name and she came over to speak to me. She was polite and friendly, but noticeably wary. This wasn't surprising and was understandable. She had probably, like me, been badly hurt and (in her mind) had probably (mistakenly) felt rejected by me.

We started with a bit of small talk. I recollect her saying "you never married did you?". I replied dryly "well you can't rush these things and I am only 50". She broke into a big smile. It was more like the old days. She was always amused by my jokes and sense of humour. She also suggested meeting up sometime, but I had just one higher priority on my mind.

I wasn't going to miss the opportunity to put the record straight and resolve all issues. This time I spoke the truth, with compassion and without looking for any personal gain (I didn't want my ego to create further problems). The right words just came out, as though directed by a higher power.

I explained that at that party (in 1978), I had merely been telling another girl that I didn't want to dance with her. I had told the other lady that I didn't want to dance with her at least three or four times and had even explained to her that it was because Olivia was there. I then said to Olivia "you were the only one who ever mattered to me and that has always been the case".

I have no doubt Olivia was very shocked. She looked at the floor, appeared to be visibly shaken, paused for a few moments and said quietly, slowly and sheepishly, but very firmly "why didn't you say something?". The way she said it left me in no doubt whatsoever that she had also wanted me very badly. We had both been desperate to be together again and so much hurt and suffering for us both could have been avoided.

Her response was so simple, but so profound! By finally speaking the truth I had dispelled the "mistaken appearance" (illusions) in her mind that I didn't care about her.

Why hadn't I said anything? A lack of confidence and a mind fearful of further hurt was the answer. If only I had known then how to overcome my fear. Resolving what had become an insurmountable problem in my mind was actually very simple. I had just needed to speak the truth. The world of hurt and fear, created by my mind, could and should have been transformed into a beautiful, pure and positive world.

I did respond to her question. Without any anger or judgment I referred to her having a few dates with a former friend and said the first thing that came to mind. I said something like "there seemed to be some bad feeling arising". It would probably have been more accurate to say "I had been hurt so badly, I just couldn't risk any more pain" and if required elaborated further. However, that didn't come to mind.

I had now completed my task with Olivia. I simply wished her well and left. Hopefully, all real and perceived issues between us were now resolved and we could both have peace of mind to assist and improve the rest of our lives.

I now had access to wisdom. Back in 1979 there was no wisdom or relevant experience to draw from and there seemed to be no escape from my prison. I felt under attack from those who were negative and hostile towards me, not to mention Nick hitting on Olivia and other friends abandoning me. I had now escaped from my prison and I had a map to a better place.

I bumped into Olivia again soon afterwards. It was at the cinema and she was bright and friendly. She even introduced me to her daughter and pointed out her husband, who was buying refreshments. She then rushed off, so as not to miss any of the film. It was a bit of an odd experience and made me think that we could easily have had a family together. However, it wasn't to be.

This again was quite a co-incidence. I hadn't seen Olivia for nearly twenty-five years and now I had seen her twice in a few months. I was sure that the time was now right and that we would continue to meet to help each other fulfil our respective life's purposes.

Interestingly, our first recent meeting in 2005 had occurred within a few months of committing to the serious study of Buddha Dharma (wisdom), Dharma being the Buddha's teachings. Again, was this a coincidence?

As I reflect on the problems we had in 1978 and 1979, I think how easy it would have been for us to get back together with the practice of **compassion**. My self-cherishing mind was full of hurt and the fear of more pain. If I had been able to generate a compassionate mind, I would have only been concerned with finding a solution to Olivia's hurt and suffering, without giving any thought to my own.

In considering and focusing only on a genuine wish to completely eradicate Olivia's pain, rather than dwelling on my own, a full reconciliation would have been inevitable and could have been effected easily. In so doing, by focusing on Olivia's hurt, I would not have given any power to my own. If you don't dwell on suffering, then you don't identify with it and don't give it any power. My own suffering would simply have disappeared and we could have resumed our love affair.

This is similar to the statement that to achieve enlightenment, the result of a totally pure and happy mind, we need to change the object of cherishing from ourselves to others. This is the Buddhist practice of "exchanging self with others".

The Power of Truth

What made this meeting special was using the power of a "declaration of truth". By reflecting on this meeting I have thought about all those many moments and opportunities where, back in 1979, I could just as easily have resolved all issues. Unfortunately, my negative minds of hurt, fear of more pain, uncontrolled desires and pride had prevailed with catastrophic results.

This meeting made me think of the film "Sliding Doors". Back then, had I taken the necessary corrective action, Olivia and I would have been reunited easily and our lives would have been very different. There were so many opportunities to do this, but each time I had instinctively chosen to avoid the possibility of more suffering rather than to grasp the mettle. Fear had made me choose to escape from the darkness of further pain, rather than to move towards the light of love. We could have enjoyed a great relationship together and we both would have been spared so much anguish, hurt and suffering.

However, the above romantic notion, while undoubtedly true, wouldn't necessarily have led to a "happy ever after" ending. These endings only occur in fairy tales and with a state of enlightenment. I'm sure we could have enjoyed as good a long term relationship as anyone can, for our love for one another was certainly very strong. Unfortunately, in samsara problems and suffering are inevitable.

Samsara, is the negative and uncontrolled mind, most of us have. Its nature is suffering and it is the result of a negative and impure, mind and life. In samsara problems would still have been inevitable. Mixed with our deep love was strong desirous attachment, this alone would have led to some suffering. Uncontrolled desires will always lead to problems.

I also needed to learn how to let go of my fear, lack of confidence and pride. Could we have changed our destiny and fate? Did we need to play out the law of cause and effect, our karma?

I am sure we could have had a good and very different life together. However, there are no guarantees in samsara. At the very least we would have endured the inevitable sufferings of ageing, sickness and death. Also, at some stage one of us would have had to deal with being parted from the other, if only because of death. Who knows what would have transpired and I had many lessons to learn.

Current Lifestyle and Career

The last few years have been diverse and interesting. Not necessarily exciting, but equally with no significant problems or worries.

I now study Buddha's teachings seriously, most Sunday afternoons and evenings. Since 2006 I have also been teaching Buddhist meditation classes, usually for two evenings per week. This enables me to deepen my own understanding.

Being self employed is really a lifestyle decision. I earn a comfortable and reasonable living from my company "FD Services", which provides services as a part time Financial Director and Freelance Financial Controller. Fortunately, all my clients are local and I now have time to devote to studying Dharma (Buddha's teachings), teaching Dharma and meditation, playing tennis and racquetball, watching football and socialising with a few valued friends.

I now try to practise humility, patient acceptance, contentment and the other Buddhist practices. Most of my holidays in recent years have been at Buddhist festivals. By trying to generate inner peace, I should have everything I need in life.

I find now many negative minds, such as anger, rarely trouble me. Anger is regarded as one of the three main poisons we need to get out of our system. It is like temporary madness, destroys our happiness, is damaging to health, harms relationships and basically serves no useful purpose whatsoever. However, there are still some negative minds to be worked on.

Now, looking back over my life, I find it difficult to believe I had so much real and suppressed anger when I was younger. Unfortunately, I still have other negative states of mind which harm my inner peace. It is these that I need to practise reducing and eliminating. Everyone is different, but my most damaging "delusions" are pride and attachment. Oh, to be able to have a calm, peaceful mind whatever the circumstances. Hopefully, one day I will be able to achieve this.

My long-standing clients have all performed well and have been successful. At the time of writing, the client I have been advising for the longest period, selling to the construction industry, in a very tough recessionary market, has outperformed competitors and suppliers. Another important client for over five years has been a major success, growing rapidly, before being sold to a larger competitor. The major shareholder is now very wealthy.

I have established and run many referral and networking groups over the years. This has helped provide me with work and has enabled me to continue to learn many new skills. This work has also provided me with many friends like Sarah and Melvin. I am also constantly meeting like-minded business people who have similar spiritual interests and values.

As I have done many times in the past, with other people, I introduced my brother Cab to his future wife Kasia (Kate) in 2004. Kasia is a sport-loving Polish girl who got an English degree to enable her to teach English. On one of her trips to England, with a couple of her university pals, she stayed with a friend of mine "Uncle" John.

Uncle John called me one day and said "I've got three beautiful Polish girls staying with me and one of them wants to play tennis, can you give her a game?". Kasia and I started playing regularly and I helped her with her dissertation. As a "thank you", she offered to take me on a tour of southern Poland.

When I returned home, Kasia said she had passed her degree and wanted to live in England for a year in order to improve her English further. I asked Cab if he would let her stay at his apartment. I gave him a "carrot", by saying "how would you like to put up a young attractive Polish girl". As usual, Cab wasn't too excited and just said "so long as it's not for too long".

The rest is history. Cab and Kasia were engaged and married within two years. The wedding reception was in a vegetarian restaurant in Krakow, on a really hot summer day. Krakow is beautiful and it was a great event, tarnished only by the drunken British stag party in our hotel.

Cab and Kasia are now happily married and she is also now a devout Baggies fan. I'm sure this "condition" would have been included in the marriage vows, which couldn't be understood as they were in Polish.

In 2008 Geoff and Anne, from Toronto, invited me to holiday there. In turn their oldest, lovely daughter Naomi invited me to her wedding in Chicago. We had a great time in both cities. It's good that nearly twenty years after working in Toronto, I still have such good friends there. I also managed to catch up with my former IT Manager colleague Betty-Ann. What a pity we live so far apart, but it's always good to hear from them all.

Life is now very good. Even my beloved football team the Baggies have established themselves in the Premiership and their future looks bright.

Olivia the final Chapter? (2009)

I had one further meeting with Olivia. I was on my way to a client and I popped in to a local town to get a problem with my mobile phone fixed.

I spotted Olivia in the high street, about 20 or 30 yards away, so I called out her name. This time she turned around with a big beaming smile and came straight over to talk. It was very pleasant. This was the Olivia that I had fallen in love with all those years ago. I think we both felt very comfortable and at ease in each others' company. As we talked the mutual respect and affection for one another was apparent.

My "declaration of truth" at our previous meeting had worked. After a while she said she had to go because her parking ticket would soon no longer be valid. I gave her my card and we said it would be good to meet for a coffee sometime. Basically, that left the ball in her court.

Olivia then came very close; she was virtually in my intimate zone and said "I really can't believe you could have possibly thought that I could possibly have had any bad feelings towards you". She had clearly been stewing over the conversation from our previous meeting a few years earlier. I just smiled because the perception of events in our minds had been so different.

Messing around with my former friend Nick, while she was very upset and believed I didn't care about her, had been very damaging. I had allowed it to create the doubt that she had "lost it", might be seeking some sort of perverted revenge and that she may be trying to hurt me.

My mind had been mistaken, but the resultant fear of more hurt had prevented me contacting her. I needn't have worried and I should have ignored my fear. This illusory, "mistaken appearance" to my mind, changed both our lives and prevented us renewing our relationship which, I now had no doubt whatsoever, is what we both had craved for.

I then offered my hand. It was intended to be a handshake, as businessmen do, to simply wish her well. She stared at my hand and I couldn't understand why. Rather than give a traditional handshake, she then held my hand in what I took as a sign of affection and respect. There was a genuine warmth between us and it was a good way to part.

I haven't seen Olivia since. Maybe we don't need to meet again. Our teacher continues to always be in front of us. Maybe we have both learnt all the lessons that we need on our respective journeys.

I now have no doubt that Olivia and myself had both been crazy about each other all along, had wanted each other very much, but had both suffered significantly and unnecessarily because of fear in our minds and perceptions that were illusory and far removed from reality. Pride was also a problem for me and probably also for her. This could all have been resolved with good, effective communication.

I will always retain great fondness for Olivia, with absolutely no negativity. All the events surrounding her have also helped create the man I am today. This is true of both the good and bad characteristics and qualities. Sometimes things have to get really bad in order to improve. This is probably true of my life.

In the past I had harboured great resentment towards Nick. His action (of betrayal) in hitting upon Olivia, as soon as he knew she was upset and believed I didn't care about her, was principally what had hurt most. It had also created a mind fearing more hurt and had created an invisible, but very real, obstacle to Olivia and I being reunited. I have no doubt that this reunion is what we both had wanted.

This action had been devastating and damaging to Olivia and to me. We could have been together in the long term, but now had separate lives and commitments without each other. In short, I had missed out on my perfect (life-long) partner. I felt

Nick had interfered in two people's lives, causing significant loss and great hurt.

Our lives had been changed considerably and I had blamed Nick. I believed that no enemy could have hurt me more. However, the real enemy had been my (uncontrolled) mind of hurt, blame, fear of more pain, excessive cravings, pride and resentment. Unfortunately, these negative states of mind had only harmed me and prevented a reconciliation with Olivia.

There had been a battle in my mind between love and fear. Unfortunately, the negative forces of fear had beaten the positive forces of love in all the early battles. I needed to make sure that in any future battles love would be victorious and fear needed to be vanquished to the past.

The action of Nick was simply part of the inescapable and inevitable "first dart" of existence. The "second dart", the one I threw myself, was how my mind reacted negatively. The actual truth was that I had suffered because my mind was uncontrolled and I was ignorant of how to resolve my issues with Olivia. My years of suffering had actually been self induced.

I wish I had had a life with Olivia. Indeed, as I review my entire life, this is the only significant regret I have. However, dwelling on the past, inevitably only brings more suffering as its companion. I know I need to continue to work on letting go of all these feelings and thoughts.

Now I have much to be grateful for and the wisdom I have found provides a toolbox for dealing with all life's problems. I certainly find life very easy now. It would have been nice to have had access to wisdom when I was young. Youth really is wasted on the young! However, I'm lucky to have found access to wisdom at all.

Maybe suffering is a gift and is necessary to learn all our life lessons. My journey is certainly continuing.

Samsara in Action 2011

Although life is generally good these days, I still get a few reminders to keep me on my spiritual path. Samsara, the world of an uncontrolled and negative mind and life, will ensure there are always difficulties presented.

It is simply no use relying on trying to control the external world to provide happiness. The external world will simply never be exactly as we want it. We will always have to endure the sufferings of birth, sickness, ageing and death, not being able to fulfil our wishes, being separated from those we love, getting what we don't want etc.

This time it was the turn of Cab and Kasia to suffer. In May 2011 Kasia gave birth to a beautiful baby girl Anuszka (Annie). Unfortunately, my little niece had a fairly common bacteria, that on rare occasions can cause severe problems. Annie developed breathing difficulties, this led to brain damage and after about ten hours of her brief existence the parents were advised to turn off the life support system.

The grief was terrible. At the funeral, Kasia sang and played guitar on a haunting song she had written herself. There wasn't a dry eye in the place as she repeated the chorus again and again "we'll never forget you, never regret you...". It displayed all the pain and passion of a grieving mother.

Two months later Kasia was made redundant from the new job she loved. Soon after that a clique appeared in the volleyball team she managed leading to rows and a huge split. There was little thanks for all the hard work she had put in, from which others had also benefitted. The negativity spread quickly and got very personal. It was very upsetting for her and culminated in her having a very difficult year.

Now, one year later (in 2012) Kasia is again pregnant. Soon I will have another niece or nephew, but for sure we'll have another junior Baggie in the family. Unfortunately, Cab now has a badly broken and very painful wrist, the result of falling over while playing Kasia at tennis.

These are all permanent reminders that to be happy we need to learn to control the mind and to keep it calm and peaceful, whatever the circumstances. Otherwise, we'll permanently live in a samsaric world fluctuating between excitement and despondency. Unless we can control our minds to generate inner peace, we'll just fluctuate between happiness and unhappiness, depending upon our external circumstances.

Goodbye Gaz (2011/12)

On Christmas Eve 2011 I popped into the Halesowen shopping centre, when I suddenly heard Gaz shout one of my nicknames "Garry", "Fleet" or "Neck". It was good to see Gaz as I hadn't seen him for a few years.

It was a very warm and friendly meeting. Gaz was busy raising a family back in 1979, when I had all my problems and lost most of my friends. However, I'm sure Gaz would have risen above it and stayed loyal. Even though I hadn't seen much of him in recent years, of all my friends and contacts, I still felt he was one of the few people who I could turn to if the chips were down. I had no doubt that Gaz would be there and would always stay loyal, if called upon.

We talked affectionately about meeting up again. We joked about our ageing and snowy haired appearance. I call my hair colour "arctic blond". I needed to leave quickly because it was my niece Danielle's birthday. We said our farewells and I touched his arm and said "make sure we do meet up soon, otherwise one of us will be turning up at the other's funeral with regrets".

It was intended as a harmless joke about our ageing. Surprisingly, Gaz gave me an odd look, which I will never forget. Gaz partly smiled at the joke, but he also gave me a serious look as he looked deeply into my eyes. I didn't know it then, but those words were very prophetic.

There has only been one other look that I have received like it in my entire life. That was when I led Fatima to her impending death. It was a look that demonstrated the depth of respect and trust, but it was tinged with sadness.

I never knew it, but Gaz had been having suicidal thoughts. I waited for the next few weeks for Gaz to get in touch with a date to meet but the message never came. Then in late January I got an unexpected call from Ben. Gaz had committed suicide. He had hanged himself from a nearby motorway bridge.

Apparently, Gaz's daughter Kelly had found the police on the motorway bridge and knew instinctively what had happened. Ann said Kelly wouldn't normally go that way and couldn't understand why she did so. Is this another co-incidence?

I went to the funeral and acted as a coffin bearer, on what would have been Gaz's fifty-eighth birthday. Ben gave one of the speeches and talked about how there was always the three of us together, "always just the three of us".

I sat behind Ann and Gaz's three grown up children. There were so many stories of his teenage years and of all the pranks and practical jokes he played, so many reminders of our friendship while growing up together. I sobbed continuously and left the service still crying with very red eyes. As I left Ann noticed immediately the state I was in and threw her arms around me.

The place was absolutely packed out, but of all the men there I was the most emotional. This is a major change, because I don't think I ever shed a tear between being a teenager until I was in my forties. In the past I simply buried and suppressed any negative feelings. When my father had died, when I was thirty eight, I didn't show any emotion at all. However, it was very different now.

Gaz's death was one of the most difficult occasions in my life to deal with and it had a profound effect on me. It helped me get things into perspective. It had the same effect as the meditations on death and impermanence. Buddhists are told to meditate on the true statement "I may die today", rather than the untrue hope "I won't die today" i.e. we always choose to put death out of our minds. Inevitably, death will occur and it may well be today.

This was a reminder for me that I needed to use the remainder of my life effectively and meaningfully. Previous objectives such as ambition, career, building businesses and trying to maximise my earnings would now take even less prominence.

One of the first things I did after Gaz's funeral was to meet up with Bill. Those few real friends who would always be loyal now assumed even more importance. I didn't want to have any more regrets about other close friends.

Bill's second wife has recently joined my sports club and become my veteran mixed doubles partner. Bill should be joining soon, after cutting down on his work. It'll be good to have good and genuine friends nearby.

As I write I have just bumped into Gaz's widow Ann. We have just reminisced over Gaz's life and I hope Ann will start attending my meditation classes, with her daughter Kelly. I have talked to Ann about how meditation will help her grieving process and how problems are smaller after meditation. Meditation won't eradicate the problem, but it will ensure the mind reacts more positively, focusing attention on other matters, resulting in less suffering.

8

The Future
Going for Refuge

"Love conquers all". However, when mixed with attachment, suffering will occur. Similarly, uncontrolled desires and wishing to gain personally, will not lead to happiness. Ego only causes division, while problems only exist in a negative mind.

As a young man, I had been very nervous and full of fear. My objective then had merely been the survival strategy of making sure I couldn't get hurt any more. In putting so many protective layers around myself I was stopping love getting in, as well as an early reconciliation with Olivia.

My ego, fear, hurt, pride and other negative minds had prevailed when I was young. But now, although I have lost the great love of my life, in the sense that we have not been together, I still feel that love prevails. I have had an excellent reconciliation, which will ensure there is no bad feeling on either side. Also, we both now know, without any doubt whatsoever, that we will both have only fond, respectful and positive thoughts of each other in the future.

Although we haven't been together for many years, now I will continue to always think fondly of Olivia and allow my mind to be full of love. As I do this, hopefully there will also be room in my heart for others.

My spiritual journey is now continuing through life, with the help of Buddha Dharma. Dharma literally means (supreme) protection (from suffering and problems). However, for these purposes Dharma should be considered to be Buddha's teachings. I have been studying Eastern philosophies since 1995. This led me to meditation and Buddhism and I have been studying Dharma seriously since 2004. I now study Dharma in a class for four and a half hours most Sundays and have been teaching meditation and Dharma since 2006, for one or two evening classes most weeks.

Dharma, meditation and the various classes keep me far more calm, peaceful and relaxed. I am a great believer in the quote "if I can maintain a calm and peaceful mind at all times, I will never experience any problems". Indeed I keep this quote in my wallet, as a permanent reminder of the mind I need to maintain.

There are "no problems outside the mind". Problems only exist when we allow our minds to become negative and when we dwell on (perceived) problems.

Basically, if the mind reacts negatively we have a problem. However, if the mind reacts positively to difficult circumstances, we don't have a problem. What is a problem to one person isn't a difficulty to another. Similarly, if we concentrate on something other than the (perceived) problem then it simply ceases to exist, unless and until we resume thinking about it. So whether the problem exists must depend upon the mind.

I have been able to prove the above from my own experiences. This is a scientific way to prove the benefits of meditation and practising Dharma. I now diligently meditate for a half hour every morning and for the same period most evenings. Whenever, I complete my meditation any (perceived) problems seem smaller or disappear completely. Similarly, if I miss a meditation session I know the difference and life isn't so easy or good.

Without meditation life is simply less enjoyable. I then reflect on how complicated and less enjoyable my life used to be and how I don't ever want to go back to those bad old days of negativity.

Similarly, during the Dharma class breaks at Christmas and in the summer, the difference is apparent. Again, life is simply less enjoyable and I note the anxiety and problems creeping back. Also, almost without exception, the other students in my class and those attending my classes make similar comments.

Buddha Shakyamuni saw so much suffering that he was motivated by great compassion to free all living beings from it. His teachings are about how to control the mind in order to be happy and free from suffering. This will happen on a gradual basis, or certainly that is what has happened to me. His teachings are as valid today, if not more so, than they were in Buddha's lifetime more than 2,500 years ago.

Buddhism is often referred to as a religion. However, I also regard it as a faith, philosophy and study in psychology. I once looked up the word "religion" in the dictionary. It mentioned "the worship of and subordination to a supernatural power". However, Buddha Shakyamuni was a man who attained enlightenment. Similarly, I understand that Buddha expressly stated that he didn't want to hear anyone worshiping him. For this reason there are statues of Buddha with no ears.

Whether Buddhism is a religion is questionable. However, what really matters is the wisdom it provides to help people be happy and free from suffering, through knowledge of how to control the mind. For this reason, I regard Buddhism as a study in psychology. Certainly, when reading, or studying Dharma, invariably I find myself saying "yes, that's how my mind works", as do my study (sangha) colleagues.

Philosophy means "the rational investigation of being, knowledge and right conduct", "a system of thought" and "serenity of temper". The definition of philosopher also includes "one who is patient, wise and stoical". I now try to live my life according to the Buddha's teachings and guidelines. For without living a virtuous life, based on moral discipline, there can be no calm peaceful mind to provide inner peace.

I believe there is a unity of all the major faiths and religions in the message of compassion, forgiveness, tolerance, contentment, simplicity and self discipline. Similarly, I believe wisdom can be found from a number of sources, including one's own experiences. However, I like the emphasis in Buddhism on controlling the mind in order to generate inner peace and find happiness.

For me the main difference between Buddhism and other philosophies and/or religions is that it does not place emphasis on the notion of a living god, but rather that we are responsible for our own happiness. This is empowering and provides a choice for practitioners between happiness and suffering. Ultimately suffering is optional, or at least the extent of it certainly is.

Happiness will only occur where there is inner peace. Inner peace will arise from concentration, which will only be effective given a foundation of the practice of moral discipline. Without concentration the mind will be weak and will just fluctuate between excitement and despondency, depending upon whether external circumstances are perceived to be good or bad.

I now take refuge in the "three jewels" Buddha, Dharma and Sangha. Buddha is like the doctor, Dharma (Buddha's teachings) the medicine and Sangha (good company) are like the supportive nurses. I now have few problems in my life. Over recent years they have been reduced by meditation and my refuge (wisdom). If only life could have been that simple when I was young. However, maybe I needed to know suffering in order to find a "true path".

There is a gift in adversity. How can you know the light if you haven't lived in the dark? Whenever there is adversity, I now look for the opportunity and try to keep life's correct perspective i.e. a happy, meaningful life, practising contentment, humility, patient acceptance and being in service to others etc.

My study continues and there are many of the profound teachings of Buddha that I need to fully understand. Similarly, there are many practices which I need to perfect and all my friends, family, work colleagues and other contacts provide many opportunities in practising patience, forgiveness, giving, compassion, love and so forth. All these practices lead to a calm, relaxed, peaceful and ultimately happy mind.

In the future, I will continue to go for refuge in Buddha, Dharma and Sangha. As life continues to get easier, meditation and other practices should provide solutions to any problems arising during my remaining years.

I can now look forward to the future with little or no fear. I now feel equipped to deal with the inevitable "samsaric" world of suffering and problems that an uncontrolled mind can create. The causes of pain will continue to be inevitable. Thankfully, I can now opt to minimise any suffering using (Buddha's) wisdom.

Epilogue

I have come a long way since those days in the late 1970s, when I endured my most difficult period, with a mind of fear, hurt and pride. I have largely achieved those goals to be "confident and tough" by experience, learning to control my mind to reduce any self limiting beliefs and letting go of fear. I now have access to wisdom and a new world has opened up for me with opportunities and challenges to enable me to develop further.

As I write this book in August 2012, at the age of fifty-eight, I have this week met up with Bill at a Baggies match (where else!). His second wife recently commented that I was a bit too competitive for their mixed doubles fun tennis. She reminds me of the attachments I need to drop.

I told Bill about the recent meetings with Olivia and their importance. He had been my closest and most loyal friend during those tough times. Bill listened attentively. I'm sure he approved of the outcome for us both. He said "it's all water under the bridge now, isn't it?". I nodded and thought that I'm sure our meetings had provided peace of mind for both of us.

I feel privileged to have had such a close relationship with Olivia. Even after all these years, I'm sure we now have a great mutual fondness, respect and affection for one another, that will always exist. I feel honoured that she thought so much of me, as I did of her. We can now both concentrate on these positives rather than the hurt and suffering that have been endured. I continue to think of her as a beautiful and lovely person in every respect and hope that she and her family are always happy in the future, regardless of whatever occurs in their lives.

I told Bill that he was aware of most of the events that had occurred, but that he hadn't been aware of just how many "friends" I had lost back in 1979. I said "it was an unwritten rule that when you are successful everyone wants to be your friend, but when you are at your lowest point everyone seems to want to kick you while you are down". I confirmed just how traumatic and difficult that period had been for me.

I then related the story of a friend of mine who built his business very quickly from half a million pounds to two million pounds sales turnover per annum. This occurred in about two years, largely with the help of one of the networking groups I ran. He was very popular when he appeared to be successful and was handing out referrals to grateful recipients. Unfortunately, he didn't have adequate financial control and his company was losing money, without him realising it.

The company went bust and my friend was made bankrupt losing his house and all his valuable assets. The day he was made bankrupt he says he had only £200 left. He had lost all his friends and then his brother, who he used to see most days and a neighbour called to demand repayment of all that he had left. He says he didn't want any more hassle and he just gave it to them. He now rarely sees his brother.

Bill later asked if I still saw Ben or Nick. I said I occasionally saw Ben, the last time being at Gaz's funeral. I said I didn't see Nick anymore as a result of him "hitting" on Olivia, as soon as he knew I had a problem to sort out. I then compared this situation, with Olivia mistakenly thinking I didn't care for her and being very upset, to having a broken lock (requiring repair) on the front door and on becoming aware of it, Nick immediately trying to steal my possessions and money.

Bill nodded that he understood what I was saying. Then he broke into a big smile and laughed as he said "to be honest I'd be more concerned about the money". It was typical of Bill.

Nick continues to provide many lessons that I still find the most difficult to overcome. I know I still have much work to do, but at least the guidance, plan and objective is clear. I also wish Nick and his family good health and happiness in the future. I hope one day I will be able to say Nick was my kind teacher, in providing the most valuable lessons in my life.

From another point of view my real enemy, the true troublemaker had been the negative minds of hurt, fear, pride and uncontrolled cravings within me. I must continue practising to control my mind to attain peaceful and positive states as much as possible.

I valued Bill's loyalty during the dark, tough times and he still continues to teach me that I shouldn't take myself or life too seriously.

As I continue along my spiritual journey my teacher will no doubt appear in many guises, in order to provide all the lessons required for further development.

Lessons Learnt and Recommended Practices

These are the main practices I try to implement throughout my life. Had I practised some of these back in 1979, I'm sure my problems with Olivia would have been easily resolved. Such examples are always speaking truth, dispelling pride (with humility), practising compassion and pure love (free from attachment and uncontrolled desires), not taking myself too seriously etc.

All the practices listed below will help generate positive, peaceful, happy minds that will be beneficial to ourselves and others:

1. Don't take ourselves too Seriously
- the root cause of all pain, problems and suffering is overstating our importance and dwelling on the wish for our own happiness
- paradoxically, it is the wish to be happy that causes us to be unhappy

2. Meditation and having a calm, still, peaceful mind
- helps reduce problems and get them into perspective
- improves health and relationships
- lessens effect of ego and helps enable access to wisdom

3. Practise Observing the Mind
- the first stage in controlling the Mind
- avoids identifying with negative states of Mind
- avoids giving power to negative states of Mind, enabling them to "drift away"

4. Always speak Truth, with Compassion and without looking for a Result (for oneself)
- compassion ensures we don't hurt others
- not looking for a result ensures our ego doesn't get in the way and helps enable us to act with wisdom
- honesty needs to be from thought, word and deed, starting with a pure intention
- a similar approach is to always state what the real problem is, how it makes us feel and the desired outcome, which will help all parties

5. Unconditional Love and Compassion
- focus on the wish to help and free others from suffering
- helps prevent negative, harmful minds such as Anger, Hatred and Jealousy from developing
- avoids mixing love with (self centred) attachment, which looks for a result for ourselves

6. Patient Acceptance
- accepting things the way they are
- things will often not be as we would like them to be and if we are unable to change them, being unhappy or worrying will serve no useful purpose whatsoever
- don't worry about what is not going to happen
- prevents negative minds such as Anger from devloping

7. Contentment
- be satisfied with one's inner and outer conditions
- avoids dissatisfaction with not obtaining the object of one's desires
- avoids dissatisfaction with new desires constantly replacing both fulfilled and unfulfilled desires

8. (finding and practising) Wisdom

- obtain guidance on how to be happy and free from suffering
- go for Refuge in a good teacher, his/her teachings and find good company for support
- learn about the true nature of all phenomena
- learn what is reality
- be aware that whatever appears to mind is illusory (mistaken appearance)
- find a meditation or Dharma class/group

9. always seeing our Teacher in front of us

- learn, develop and continuously improve from all of life's experiences
- be aware that all negative states of mind highlight our weaknesses
- take responsibility for all weaknesses and negative states of Mind
- see the "gift" in suffering

10. (always see) Others as "Supreme"

- don't Judge or Criticise Others
- it is easy to see faults in others, but a wise man sees the faults in himself
- always look at causes, conditions and dependent relationships
- "never judge a man until you've walked a mile in his moccasins"
- learn lessons about own weaknesses (whenever the mind is negative)
- helps avoid many negative minds which ordinarily lead to suffering

11. practise Humility to dispel Pride

- pride makes us believe we are always right
- pride prevents reconciliation and creates difficulties in relationships
- pride is a negative mind that leads to suffering
- pride "always comes before a fall"
- pride can prevent us speaking truth
- to practise humility: remind ourselves how little we really know compared to the great teachers

12. practise Gratitude (every day)

- enables us to get our perceived problems into perspective
- helps generate a positive, happy mind

Glossary

This brief glossary is not intended to provide precise definitions. Indeed it will be possible to find more comprehensive and precise definitions in Buddhist texts elsewhere. However, for the purposes of this book and to improve the understanding of the meaning I wish to convey, I suggest the following be attributed to the words listed below:

Bodhichitta: A mind of enlightenment, that wishes to benefit all living beings.

Bodhisattva: A person at a very advanced stage of awareness and close to Buddhahood, being spontaneously motivated by the mind of Bodhichitta.

Compassion: A selfless and virtuous mind wishing to free someone/others from suffering.

Contentment: To be satisfied with one's inner and outer conditions.

Desirous Attachment: A mind that exaggerates the good qualities of someone or something, mistakenly sees it/him/her as a cause of happiness, desires it/him/her and wishes to possess it/him/her. Also involves uncontrolled desires/cravings.

Dharma: Literally meaning the supreme protection (from suffering). Usually used to refer to the Buddha's teachings.

Love: A selfless and virtuous mind that is unmixed with desirous attachment and does not desire for oneself, but wishes for someone/others to be happy. Love includes the following:
- affectionate love (seeing someone/something as pleasant, likeable or beautiful)
- cherishing love (seeing someone/something as precious and important) and
- wishing love (wishing for someone/something to be happy)

Pride: A mind that exaggerates one's own importance and (perceived) good qualities. Can lead to excessive self esteem and conceit.

Samsara: The world of worries, problems, anxiety and suffering that is perceived by an uncontrolled and/or impure and/or negative mind and/or life. Also, sometimes used in the context of uncontrolled rebirth.

Wisdom: The quality of understanding the true nature of reality, free from mistaken appearances and conceptions in mind, as ultimately occurs in Buddhahood.
Conventionally, involves gaining accurate insights and understanding from experience and learning.

Dedication

This book is for everyone. May it help them find inner peace.

May everyone learn from these lessons, find the wisdom to use their lives meaningfully and be happy and free from suffering.

"Our greatest fear is not that we are inadequate. Our greatest fear is that we are powerful beyond measure". Nelson Mandela (Inaugural Speech).

About the Author

Paul Webb was born in 1954 in Birmingham, England. Apart from a couple of years in Toronto and Huddersfield, he has spent all his life living in the West Midlands.

Paul qualified as an accountant in 1982 and also has a marketing diploma. He now works as a part time finance director and freelance financial controller. He has extensive experience in business and has been self employed since 1998.

In his twenties Paul encountered tragedy. It was this suffering that inspired and motivated him to question all conventional lifestyle choices and beliefs in the causes of happiness. By experience and a process of elimination he has reviewed all traditional Western beliefs in life's priorities. Since 1995 Paul has undertaken serious study and practise in Eastern faiths, philosophies, meditation and in particular Buddhism.

It is through meditation, the above mentioned study and Buddhism that Paul has found the answers to his philosophical search.

Paul's request to you:

Please do not allow this book to gather dust. After you have read it, please pass it to someone else, so that they may also be able to find a great teacher and discover the wisdom to enable them to be happy and free from suffering.